Three-Week SAT Crash Course - Grammar

Copyright © 2021 by Chelsey M. Snyder

All rights reserved. No part of this book may be reproduced or used in any manner without written permission of the copyright owner except for the use of quotations in a book review. For more information, address: CSnyder@VohraMethod.com

FIRST EDITION

ISBN: 978-0-9992711-2-4

www.VohraMethod.com

Table of Contents

1. What to do if you have more than 3 weeks
2. How to improve your grammar score in 3 weeks
3. Free vocabulary building software & SAT quick facts
7. Learn the Basics
56. Selected Skills
115. Punctuation Skills
156. Reading Crossover
169. Test 1 Grammar Section - Crossover Questions
253. Test 2
282. The Rest of the Practice Tests

What if I have more than Three Weeks?

Wait Chelsey! What should I do if I have more than three weeks before my test? Should I just wait around until three weeks before and then start this training?

No. First of all, don't be dumb. That would be very, very stupid. Please do not do that. In fact, don't even wait for ONE DAY. Get started today.

Second, if you have more than three weeks, you should read this book, and then follow the additional training suggestions at the end of the book. The additional training can continue for however much time you have available. It just gets harder and harder until you can surpass any obstacle and you're nearly guaranteeing yourself a perfect score.

If you want a fast score boost, this book can get you there in three weeks. If you want a perfect score, the additional training will get you there in three months or more. You have to DO it, and you have to pour your heart and soul and everything into it. You should spend a lot of time on this training regardless. But, it can be done!

So, don't wait ever. Avoidance will never get you a good SAT score. Other obligations will never get you a good SAT score. Your friend's birthday party, your next three soccer matches, your piano practice, and your great aunt and uncle's wedding anniversary...will all NOT get you a good score. So, get your priorities straight and get down to business!

How to Improve Your SAT Grammar Score in Three Weeks

Read this book. Do the things the book tells you to do. Actually do them! Don't just pretend or say that you'll do it later and then forget. Answer every question yourself. Write out every exercise for the hardest problems. Take all the time it takes now so that you can be fast and reliable when you take the real test.

Accuracy comes first; speed comes second.

If you need help, contact me at www.VohraMethod.com/crash-course-resources.

Free Vocabulary Building Software and a few quick facts about the SAT

I'm going to assume, because you're reading this, that you already:

1. Think the SAT is important.
2. Want to get a perfect (or very high score).
3. Realize that the SAT is a serious challenge.
4. Want your SAT training to take as little time as possible.

I won't waste time convincing you of the above. But, I do want to add something to point number 2.

The SAT is a very formidable opponent.

This is more than a fact; it's a call to action. You must fundamentally change the way you think about the SAT if you want to get a perfect score. **First**, from this point forward, you must never utter the words, "Oh, I just made a simple mistake."

There are no "simple mistakes" on the SAT. There are just people who get paid to come up with new ways to make you get stuff wrong on the SAT...and you fell for it.

There are also no "guessing methods", and there is no such thing as "two correct answer choices, but one of them is better". All of that is nonsense, and you must get it out of your brain immediately. Those thoughts will guarantee that you **don't** get a perfect score.

Second, you must immediately throw your calculator off a balcony, into the trash, or into the backpack of your worst enemy. Calculators will make you exactly the kind of button-punching monkey that can only achieve mediocrity on the SAT.

"Quickly trying out all the answers" is not an approach that will work for a perfect score, or even a 1500+. It's just slow nonsense that will create more stress as it eats up all of your time. Even worse, it indicates that there is some fundamental piece of Algebra that you don't know. You can't just let yourself not know those pieces of Algebra. You must fill in those gaps quickly and permanently. Then, you won't need a calculator anyways.

"But Chelsey, isn't this the grammar book?"

"Yes. And throwing out your calculator will change the way you think about the entire SAT as a whole."

Start good mental habits right away.

Your First Good Habit: Study Vocabulary every day!

If you already have a system for studying vocabulary, use that. If you don't, we'll get you set up with our Vocabulary Synapse software that we offer to everyone completely free because we know how important vocabulary is to your success.

Several questions on the SAT Reading and Grammar directly test your vocabulary knowledge. BUT! They almost always pick a word with multiple meanings...and then list ALL those meanings as your four answer choices.

Alternatively, they will just pick a word that's hard and you either know it or you don't.

Several other questions on the SAT Reading indirectly test your vocabulary by requiring evidence that has dense vocabulary in it. If you don't understand that sentence in the passage, you're going to get the question AND the evidence question wrong. And it was all an issue of vocab...

On the SAT Grammar section, they are also testing your reading ability. The sentence ordering questions and other analytical writing questions in the grammar section can rely on challenging vocabulary to trip you up, in transition words and elsewhere.

Vocab is important. It's also easy to study with our free Vocab Synapse program.

Set up a free consultation today at www.VohraMethod.com and we'll get you set up with access to your free daily vocab training.

However you do it, you must study vocabulary every single day! Just start with 20 minutes per day, then move up to about 30 minutes. You can study in the car, on a bus, on a plane, or during your boring, irrelevant school classes. It doesn't matter when you do it, just do it.

Your Second Good Habit: Laughter

In order to do well on the SAT, the number one thing you need is someone to look at the mistakes you've made and jovially laugh at you.

But Chelsey, getting laughed at doesn't sound fun…

Well, taking the SAT isn't a party either. The point is that you don't just need to be told what you did wrong. You need to get into a place where you can laugh at yourself for the ridiculous answers and mistakes you're making. Only then will you really change.

If you can't afford a private tutor, just laugh at yourself when you mess up. If you can, come work with me.

Laughter is also uplifting and healing. You don't need to wallow in the grief of your first SAT attempt, or your first practice test score. You need to overcome that first score. Laughter is a positive way to train the brain to stop making lazy, ridiculous errors.

Most students come into our courses and our private sessions carrying a lot of emotional baggage. "I'm terrible at tests." "I always do poorly on the math section." "My parents and I have been fighting about this stupid test for months."

Whatever your emotional baggage is, put it on the next flight to Mars and don't look back. Everything you've done so far, all the worrying and bickering and wallowing and nonsense, got you to where you are now. If you don't want to stay where you are now, then you need to do something different.

Learn the Basics

First off, many students come in to see me and have never been taught formal grammar in their lives. Some students come in and haven't seen grammar since 1st grade, and even then, it was very, very minimal.

I have seen a ton of juniors and seniors who could not differentiate between complex nouns and verbs.

Vocab Synapse will help with this! When you're learning the definitions, you'll know if a word is a noun or a verb. From there, you'll start to pick up on all the noun and verb endings.

Most importantly, if this is your situation, remember it is not your fault. **Your school failed you. YOU did not fail.** You should feel absolutely no guilt or shame about this.

But you do have to rise above it.

Some of this process will feel like "little kids' stuff", but you have to go through it. You've got to know grammar for the grammar section, reading section, and regular life (reading and writing). Businesses don't like to hire people who can't write English good.

Nouns, Verbs, Adjectives, Adverbs

I assume you're pretty familiar with the following, but I have had students who were a bit shaky on their core grammar. Grammar is not taught in schools almost country-wide at this point, sadly, so it's not your fault. Just a few pages of review.

A noun is a person, place, thing, or idea. Nouns don't really get complicated until you get into ideas.

Verbs are actions.

Adjectives tell you stuff about nouns (they describe). They answer the questions WHO and WHAT.

Adverbs tell you stuff about verbs (also describing). They answer the questions WHEN, WHERE, WHY, and HOW.

A lot of English words will pull from the same roots. You can have a noun, adjective, and verb that all look very similar.

Attention (noun)
Attentive (adjective)
Attend (verb)

Communication (noun)
Communicative (adjective)
Communicate (verb)

The easiest way to tell them apart is through their word endings (suffixes).

Common Noun Endings: -tion, -ity, -er, -ness, -ism, -ment, -ant, -ship, -age, -ery

Common Verb Endings: -en, -ise/-ize, -ate, -ify/-fy, -ed (past tense)

Common Adjective Endings: -able/-ible, -al, -ant, -ary, -ful, -ic, -ous, -ive, -y

Common Adverb Endings: -ly

These are just the common ones, but they can help you a lot.

Practice: Identify the bolded words below as noun, verb, adjective, or adverb.

It is not thus that the Americans understand that **species** of democratic equality which may be **established** between the sexes. They admit, that as nature has **appointed** such wide differences between the physical and moral **constitution** of man and woman, her **manifest design** was to give a **distinct employment** to their various **faculties**; and they hold that **improvement** does not **consist** in **making beings** so **dissimilar** do pretty nearly the same things, but in getting each of them to **fulfill** their **respective tasks** in the best **possible** manner. The Americans have **applied** to the sexes the great **principle** of political economy which **governs** the **manufactures** of our age, by **carefully** dividing the **duties** of man from those of woman, in order that the great work of society may be the better carried on.

This passage is from an SAT Reading passage, and it was originally published in 1840.

Answers:

It is not thus that the Americans understand that **species (noun)** of democratic equality which may be **established (verb)** between the sexes. They admit, that as nature has **appointed (verb)** such wide differences between the physical and moral **constitution (noun)** of man and woman, her **manifest (adjective) design (noun)** was to give a **distinct (adjective) employment (noun)** to their various **faculties (noun)**; and they hold that **improvement (noun)** does not **consist (verb)** in **making (trick question, actually a noun. It's called a Gerund! We'll learn more about this later) beings (noun)** so **dissimilar (adjective)** do pretty nearly the same things, but in getting each of them to **fulfill (verb, infinitive)** their **respective (adjective) tasks (noun)** in the best **possible (adjective)** manner. The Americans have **applied (verb)** to the sexes the great **principle (noun)** of political economy which **governs (verb)** the **manufactures (noun)** of our age, by **carefully (adverb)** dividing the **duties (noun)** of man from those of woman, in order that the great work of society may be the better carried on.

Subjects & Direct Objects

The most important part of any sentence (or clause) in the world is the VERB. When in doubt, look for the verb, always.

After that, you can find the subject.

The Subject is the noun that performs the action.

Fred hit the ball. (hit is the verb; Fred is the Subject)

Obviously, the subject isn't always very easy to find. But, if you can find the subject and the verb, you will know about 80% of the meaning of the sentence. (80% is not enough comprehension to get a perfect score, obv. It's also not enough comprehension to get a 1500+ SAT/33+ ACT. However, it is a start.)

Once you find the Subject and Verb, look for the Direct Object.

The Direct Object is the noun that receives the action. There is NOT a Direct Object in every sentence.

Fred hit the ball. (hit is the verb; the ball is the thing that got hit, aka the Direct Object)

Not every sentence has a DO, but if the sentence does, then you increase your comprehension of that sentence (or clause) to around 90%. (90% is still not close enough for a perfect score or a 1500+/33+. Those scores are the top 1%, and they require top 1% skills. Thus, you need 99% accuracy in order to achieve a 1500 or a 33.)

Again, not all Direct Objects are easy to find, but we'll start easy.

Also, remember this is a crash course. I'll tell you the most fundamental things that you need to know. If you want more information, feel free to browse the internet or set up a session with me. We can talk at length about these concepts, but we don't need to. You just need to internalize them as simple, core ideas, and you'll be golden!

Practice: Identify the Verb first! Then the Subject. Then the Direct Object (if there is one).

1. The tall man has a shadow.
2. The birds carried GPS devices.
3. The volcano caused global cooling.
4. The gold had kept his thoughts in an ever-repeated circle.
5. The influence must gather force with every new year.
6. Shapes and sounds grew clearer for Ellie's eyes and ears.

Order really does make a difference when finding these things. Always look for the verb first.

Shortly, I'll show you long phrases and clauses that can stack together to make a sentence very long, AND that contain a lot of verbs or things that look like verbs. This means that finding the MAIN verb will be no simple task. If you find "the verb" but it's actually inside of a noun clause…then that wasn't the main verb. It'll make more sense in a bit.

Key:

VERBS
Subjects
{Direct Objects}

Answers:

1. The tall **man** HAS a {shadow}.
2. The **birds** CARRIED gps {devices}.
3. The **volcano** CAUSED global {cooling}.
4. The **gold** HAD KEPT (two-part verb) his {thoughts} in an ever-repeated circle.
5. The **influence** MUST GATHER {force} with every new year.
6. **Shapes and sounds** GREW clearer for Eppie's eyes and ears. {no DO}

You'll notice that there are often words in between the verb and the direct object. This is NOT a rule, there are often not words in between. I mention them because those are adjectives. They modify the DO, but they are not, themselves, the Direct Object.

You'll also see several words after the Direct Objects in the last three sentences. Those are prepositional phrases, which we'll learn next. They are one of the MOST common things found in English sentences… they're everywhere!

Prepositional Phrases

Prepositional phrases are always modifiers. They can be adjectives or adverbs, but they are not nouns or verbs. They are also easy to identify.

Prepositional phrases start with a preposition and end with a noun, the FIRST noun that you find after the preposition.

Examples of prepositions:

of, at, with, on, in, to, from, into, by, off, upon

also

next to, beyond, beside, without, inside, outside, behind, in front of, around

So, lots of prepositions will be pretty small words. **That's trouble because you all often like to ignore the smallest words. So…don't!**

Prepositions generally show a physical/spatial relationship. Back in grade school, I was taught to think of all the things a mouse could be in relation to a box. It could be on the box, in the box, under the box, next to the box, at the box; it could walk to the box or away from the box, etc. That doesn't cover every preposition, but it helps. You'll recognize these more and more.

Practice:

Find the preposition, and then find the very first noun after that preposition. You will have found the complete prepositional phrase.

1. The penguin with the hat waddled.
2. The boy with the orange carrot likes dogs.
3. The alligator floated in the lazy river.
4. The tall tree strongly resisted the wind.
5. The umbrella with stripes broke.
6. The ballerina danced on the stage.
7. The man bought the toy on the highest shelf.
8. The man excitedly shouted at his friend.
9. The song unexpectedly ended.
10. The car drove over the new bridge.
11. The woman was standing with a happy, jumping, singing, juggling bear.

Answers:

1. The penguin [with the hat] waddled.
2. The boy [with the orange carrot] likes dogs.
3. The alligator floated [in the lazy river].
4. The tall tree strongly resisted the wind. [none]
5. The umbrella [with stripes] broke.
6. The ballerina danced [on the stage].
7. The man bought the toy [on the highest shelf].
8. The man excitedly shouted [at his friend].
9. The song unexpectedly ended. [none]
10. The car drove [over the new bridge].
11. The woman was standing [with a happy, jumping, singing, juggling bear].

Clauses

There are several types of clauses. Clauses differ from phrases in that phrases NEVER contain any verbs of any kind and **clauses MUST contain a subject and verb**.

Independent vs Dependent

Independent Clause: This is described as "a clause that can stand on its own". This just means that it could, **independently** be a real sentence.

Dependent Clause: Could not be its own sentence.

Independent: I ate the banana.

Dependent: Even though I ate the banana,

Notice that the dependent clause doesn't finish a complete thought. If someone said that to you out loud, you would keep silent and wait for them to finish their sentence. That's the idea.

Practice Level 1:

Decide if the underlined portion is Independent or Dependent.

1. Fred went to school, and <u>he ate a fish</u>.

2. Fred saw the man <u>who ate a fish</u>.

3. <u>When I was seven</u>, I went to the zoo.

4. <u>Although I am going to go to school and then go to work</u>, I will have time.

5. <u>What I want</u> is a car.

6. <u>Because the weather changed so many times throughout the day</u>, we had to call and cancel our plans!

7. While our plans were being changed, <u>my friend found hundreds of reasons to complain and regret lost opportunities</u>.

8. <u>Tensions were high</u> when we finally got to our new destination.

9. Everyone was ready for a long day of rest, <u>although we hadn't done much of anything all day</u>!

Answers:

1. Independent
2. Dependent
3. Dependent
4. Dependent
5. Dependent
6. Dependent
7. Independent
8. Independent
9. Dependent

Practice Level 2:

Decide if the entire thing is Independent or Dependent.

1. Because consumers reap the nutritional benefits of Greek yogurt and support those who make and sell it.

2. Most of Greenland's interior is covered by a thick layer of ice and compressed snow.

3. I found myself feeling isolated.

4. Therefore, farmers and businesses should continue finding safe and effective methods of producing the food.

5. While falling as particles onto the ice sheet.

6. When I left my office job as a website developer at a small company for a position that allowed me to work full-time from home.

Answers:

1. Dependent
2. Independent
3. Independent
4. Independent
5. Dependent
6. Dependent

Those were all pulled from SAT grammar sections. Those are exactly the types of tricks they like to pull. One answer choice will make the sentence be like number 6, a very long fragment, misleading because of its length. They'll hope that, because it's long, you won't notice that it started with a word like "because" or "when" or "although" or "while". Those words, btw, all generally introduce Dependent Clauses (also "as" and "yet").

You may have noticed, also, that "therefore" CAN be the start of an Independent clause, as seen in number 4. It can also start a Dependent clause. So, don't solely use key words to make your decisions. Read and think. Ask yourself if the "sentence" is actually a sentence at all.

Practice Level 3:

1. Here's a rule: A sentence has to have at least ONE Independent Clause. You can't make a sentence out of Dependent Clauses; that would be called a Fragment!

   Knowing that, how would you fix the bolded portion?

   Because consumers reap the nutritional benefits of Greek yogurt and support those who make and sell **it, therefore farmers** and businesses should continue finding safe and effective methods of producing the food.

2. Here's another fun rule: When you join two Independent Clauses, you use {comma} AND, {comma} BUT, {comma} OR. Sometimes you can use a semicolon.

   When you join a Dependent Clause and an Independent clause, you're usually going to use ONLY a comma. No AND, no BUT, no OR (those are called conjunctions).

   Knowing that, how would you correct the bolded portion below?

   While these classes are particularly helpful to young students developing basic research skills, **but** adult patrons can also benefit from librarian assistance in that they can acquire job-relevant computer skills.

       (A) NO CHANGE
       (B) and
       (C) for
       (D) DELETE the underlined portion.

3. Because digital systems record ★ **indiscriminately; they** ★ cannot discern important parts of the proceedings from other noises in the courtroom.

    (A) NO CHANGE
    (B) indiscriminately, they
    (C) indiscriminately. They
    (D) indiscriminately, therefore they

Answers:

1. You would need to take out the word "therefore".

   Here are your two clauses:

   [Because consumers reap the nutritional benefits of Greek yogurt and support those who make and sell it] **Dependent**, [therefore farmers and businesses should continue finding safe and effective methods of producing the food] **Dependent**.

   If you look at the original clauses, you can see that both of them are dependent. You can't make a sentence out of only dependent clauses. So, you need to make one of those clauses Independent. This is done by removing the word "therefore" in this case.

2. Answer is D.

   Again, you can't have two dependent clauses.

   [While these classes are particularly helpful to young students developing basic research skills] **Dependent**, [but adult patrons can also benefit from librarian assistance in that they can acquire job-relevant computer skills] **Dependent**.

3. Answer is B.

   [Because digital systems record indiscriminately] **Dependent**; [they cannot discern important parts of the proceedings from other noises in the courtroom] **Independent**.

   The first clause is Dependent; the second clause is Independent. You'll learn more about semicolons later. The big thing is that you can't separate a dependent clause from an independent one using a semicolon! Only a comma.

Adjective and Adverb Clauses

Adjective Clauses like to start with "who", "whom", "which", "that". They tell you more about WHO a character is or WHICH thing is being discussed. So, that makes some easy sense.

Adverb Clauses tell you WHY something happens, WHEN it happens, etc. So, they usually start with words like "since", "because", "although", "while", "when".

From there, both proceed to have, you guessed it, a subject and a verb, and probably some other modifiers up in there.

The difference is not just in what word they start with, though. The difference is in what sort of information they provide, and which word they modify. THAT is how you use grammar to increase your reading comprehension. You read the phrases and clauses and modifiers and stuff, and you figure out what is being modified and how that shapes the people, places, things, and actions of the story/article/passage.

Practice 1:

Identify the adjective and adverb clauses. Then, write down what word they modify.

1. The girl who was smart passed the test.
2. The man who played guitar danced on stage.
3. I ate food because I was hungry.
4. The clown who had green hair rode a bike.
5. The performer sang while he played the guitar.
6. The grass grew until I cut it.
7. The woman hit the thief who stole her purse.
8. The elephant loved the man who fed it.

Answers:

[adjective clause]
{adverb clause}
Word that the clause modifies

1. The **girl** [who was smart] passed the test.
2. The **man** [who played guitar] danced on stage.
3. I **ate** food {because I was hungry}.
4. The **clown** [who had green hair] rode a bike.
5. The performer **sang** {while he played the guitar}.
6. The grass **grew** {until I cut it}.
7. The woman hit the **thief** [who stole her purse].
8. The elephant loved the **man** [who fed it].

Practice 2:

I'm breaking this into two so that you have an opportunity to see the answers above and learn from them. Aim to get a perfect 10/10 on this set!

1. I stopped singing when the song ended.
2. When the rain poured through the window, I grabbed a mop.
3. The rose pricked the girl who touched it.
4. The man who was a farmer grew grapes.
5. The girl ate popcorn while she watched the movie.
6. I watched the comedian who won the award.
7. The astronaut who went to the moon studied science.
8. When Winter approaches, bears gain weight.
9. I ate cake because I wanted sweets.
10. The book was written by the mathematician who studied Linear Algebra.

Answers:

1. I **stopped** singing {when the song ended}. (If you got the verb wrong here, that's okay. We'll discuss gerunds later on. The short story here is that "singing" is the thing -noun- that I stopped doing. Stopped is the verb. Singing is the DO.)

2. {When the rain poured through the window}, I **grabbed** a mop.

3. The rose pricked the **girl** [who touched it].

4. The **man** [who was a farmer] grew grapes.

5. The girl **ate** popcorn {while she watched the movie}.

6. I watched the **comedian** [who won the award].

7. The **astronaut** [who went to the moon] studied science.

8. {When Winter approaches}, bears **gain** weight.

9. I **ate** cake {because I wanted sweets}.

10. The book was written by the **mathematician** [who studied Linear Algebra].

37

Noun Clauses

Noun clauses are probably the weirdest type of clause, and they're the hardest to read. They are still a clause, so they have a subject and verb, sometimes a direct object, and sometimes a bunch of modifiers too. But after ALL THAT, the noun clause is still just one noun serving a bigger purpose in the **main** sentence.

Noun clauses are always going to express ideas (because those are the complicated types of nouns). They'll look something like this:

Paul heard [what I said].

[What I did] was really funny.

Noun clauses often start with "what" or "that". **On the SAT, if you see the word "that" as the very first word in a sentence, you should look to see if it's a noun clause.** It often is.

So, it works like this:

Paul heard [what I said].

Verb: heard
Subject: Paul
DO (what is the thing that gets heard?): [what I said] is the thing that gets heard.

So, "what I said" is one, cohesive thing (noun), but it's made up of its own verb, subject, etc.

Let's practice some easier ones.

Practice (easy):

Find the main verb. Then, find the noun clause. Then, write down if it's the subject or the direct object of the **main** verb.

1. I want what everyone wants.
2. I know what you did. *(Quote from The Good Place)*
3. You kill what you eat. You eat what you kill.
4. I can't forget what I saw north of the wall. *(Quote from Game of Thrones)*
5. What I want is not important. *(Quote from Star Trek)*
6. As they run out of fuel, what I want is very important. *(Quote from Die Hard)*

Answers:

1. I want [what everyone wants]. Direct Object of "want".

2. I know [what you did]. Direct Object of "know".

3. You kill [what you eat]. You eat [what you kill]. Direct Objects of "kill" and "eat".

4. I can't forget [what I saw north of the wall]. Direct Object of "can't forget".

5. [What I want] is not important. Subject of "is".

6. As they run out of fuel, [what I want] is very important. Subject of "is".

Practice (hard):

Now we do some much harder sentences from real SAT passages. Just find **ALL** noun clauses.

1. She learned that Claude and Wilfrid were delicate, sensitive young people, that Irene had the artistic temperament highly developed, and that Viola was something or other else of a mould equally commonplace among children of that class and type in the twentieth century.

2. That half the human race is excluded by the other half from any participation in government; that they are native by birth but foreign by law in the very land where they were born; and that they are property-owners yet have no direct influence or representation: are all political phenomena apparently impossible to explain on abstract principle.

3. We further postulate that the proper dosage necessary to prevent mite infestation may be better left to the bees, who may seek out or avoid pyrethrum containing plants depending on the amount necessary to defend against mites and the amount already consumed by the bees, which in higher doses could be potentially toxic to them.

4. What I do know is that if fiscal crisis were going to drive affluent professionals out of central cities, it would have done so by now.

5. What I am on the brink of knowing, I now see, is not an ephemeral mathematical spot but myself.

6. But when Lavigne's team examined shards of volcanic glass from this volcano, they found that they didn't match the chemical composition of the glass found in polar ice cores, whereas the Samalas glass is a much closer match.

7. That a powerful volcano erupted somewhere in the world, sometime in the Middle Ages, is written in polar ice cores in the form of layers of sulfate deposits and tiny shards of volcanic glass.

Answers and Discussion:

[noun clauses]

If there are several in a row, I'll alternate bolding them and italicizing them. They are ALL noun clauses. I'm just using visual cues here.

1. She learned **[that Claude and Wilfrid were delicate, sensitive young people]**, *[that Irene had the artistic temperament highly developed]*, and **[that Viola was something or other else of a mould equally commonplace among children of that class and type in the twentieth century]**.

So, three noun clauses in a row! And, all of them are direct objects. They're all things that "she learned". She learned about Claude and Wilfred, about Irene, and about Viola. That last noun clause is pretty critical. Look at how many modifiers there are in that thing.

Viola (subj) **was** (verb) {something or other else} (DO) **[of a mould equally commonplace]** (prep phrase modifying "something or other") **[among children]** (prep phrase modifying "commonplace") **[of that class and type]** (prep phrase modifying "children") **[in the twentieth century]** (prep phrase modifying "class and type").

ALL that happening inside a noun clause… It's pretty cool, but it does make reading more complex. Especially when there are several strung together and the sentence becomes a 100-word-long monstrosity. But, you'll get the hang of it!

By the way, feel free to revisit your answers to the original questions in between each answer I give. The point here is to learn, not to get it all right on the first try. With all the love in the world, I must encourage you not to be an idiot. Successful people always realize that the only path forward is growth and action. Moping because you got one wrong is not growth, nor is it an action. Convincing yourself that you would have gotten it right but you made a "simple mistake" is also not growth or action at all. Just keep trying again. Trying is an action.

2. **[That half the human race is excluded by the other half from any participation in government]**; *[that they are native by birth but foreign by law in the very land where they were born]*; and **[that they are property-owners yet have no direct influence or representation]**: are all political phenomena apparently impossible to explain on abstract principle.

Again here, three noun clauses in a row. (I have mentioned that the SAT basically just hates you and wants you to suffer, right? Lol. Okay, I joke, but still, it's pretty rough…)

As an added bonus, and more reinforcement of what you've learned before, try to find the subject, verb, DO (if there is one), and all prepositional phrases in each noun clause.

All three of those noun clauses are subjects of the verb "are" towards the end there. This is pretty common in older styles of writing. It was one of their fancy ways of making sure that no sentence would ever be under 50 words (lol).

3. We further postulate **[that the proper dosage necessary to prevent mite infestation may be better left to the bees, who may seek out or avoid pyrethrum containing plants depending on the amount necessary to defend against mites and the amount already consumed by the bees, which in higher doses could be potentially toxic to them]**.

That whole thing is just ONE big noun clause. For this one, definitely break it down. Find verb, subject, DO (if there is one), and all prep phrases.

Answer to bonus question:

…that the proper dosage necessary to prevent mite infestation may be better left to the bees, who may seek out or avoid pyrethrum containing plants depending on the amount necessary to defend against mites and the amount already consumed by the bees, which in higher doses could be potentially toxic to them.

Verb: may be left
Subject: dosage
DO: none

Now, this was a little bit of a trick question because "to prevent" is an infinitive, not the verb here. We haven't learned infinitives yet, but we will soon.

"to prevent mite infestation" is an infinitive phrase that modifies the "proper dosage".

"to the bees" is a prep phrase that modifies the verb "may be left".

Then the entire following thing is one big, huge adjective clause modifying the bees: who may seek out or avoid pyrethrum containing plants depending on the amount necessary to defend against mites and the amount already consumed by the bees, which in higher doses could be potentially toxic to them.

Then, we can break down that adjective clause even further, verb, subject, etc.:

who may seek out or avoid pyrethrum containing plants depending on the amount necessary to defend against mites and the amount already consumed by the bees, which in higher doses could be potentially toxic to them.

Verb: may seek out or avoid
Subject: who
Direct Object: plants

Then, that clause goes on to have several prep phrases, infinitives, participles, etc. We haven't learned about some of those yet, so we can stop there for now. But, you can really see how far you can break down a sentence in order to get to the core of what's happening.

This level of engagement with a single sentence is good. There is a general principle that I want you to understand.

Imagine you watch a film one time. You'll notice the big things. The plot, the characters, maybe the setting. Then, you watch the film 15 or 20 times. You'll notice a lot more stuff: nuances in the dialogue or accents, camera angles that are used to create different moods, maybe the film score and how it develops the plot. Next, you watch the same film 100 times. By then, you're noticing the smallest details in the background and setting, lighting and blocking decisions that the director made, all sorts of stuff. You see those things because you've already noticed the bigger things.

Now here's the kicker: After you've watched that **one** movie 100 times, you'll notice all those same tiny details in every new movie you watch. You're used to them now.

The same will hold true in reading and grammar. Honestly, the reason why I'm so good at standardized tests is not that I've seen 8000 different SAT tests. The reason is that I've poured over the same 10 or so tests hundreds of times each. In fact, I tend to gravitate back to the same tests over and over when I'm looking for new ways to teach students a skill or examine an SAT trick further.

Even when new practice tests come out, I'm less interested in those than I am in the same old ones I've seen a hundred times.

But, of course, when I do see the new ones, everything I've learned time and again is immediately apparent. That's where I want you to end up.

4. *[What I do know]* is [that if fiscal crisis were going to drive affluent professionals out of central cities, it would have done so by now].

Verb: is
Subject: What I do know
That other noun clause is not the DO. It's something else called a Predicate Nominative. But, don't worry about that for now.

5. [What I am on the brink of knowing], I now see, is not an ephemeral mathematical spot but myself.

That noun clause is the subject of "is".

6. But when Lavigne's team examined shards of volcanic glass from this volcano, they found [that they didn't match the chemical composition of the glass found in polar ice cores], whereas the Samalas glass is a much closer match.

That noun clause is the Direct Object of "found".

7. [That a powerful volcano erupted somewhere in the world, sometime in the Middle Ages], is written in polar ice cores in the form of layers of sulfate deposits and tiny shards of volcanic glass.

That whole thing is the subject of "is".

Keep practicing with this on every passage and every book that you read!

Gerunds, Participles, and Infinitives, Oh my! (This is a Wizard of Oz joke.)

All of these things are important because they look exactly like verbs, but they are NOT verbs. So, when you need to find the main verb in your sentence (you know, that big 80% of the meaning) you'll need to be able to weed out all three of these.

Gerunds: Look like verbs, but they are nouns. They also end in -ing.

Participles: Look like verbs, but they are adjectives. They can end in whatever, sometimes -ing, sometimes -ed, sometimes other endings.

Infinitives: Look like verbs, but they are actually adjectives, nouns, or even adverbs. They always start with "to".

Let's dive a bit deeper.

Gerunds

You might say, "I like cookies." You might also say, "I like hiking." ("Hiking" is a gerund.)

In the first sentence, the DO is "cookies". In the second sentence, the DO is "hiking".

Student: But, "hiking" looks like a verb!

Me: Yes, that's the point.

Hiking is often a verb, as in "I went hiking". But, you can also use it like a noun. You can talk about the idea or concept of hiking. Again, this is primarily important for helping you determine the main verb in the main clause of a sentence.

Participles

In a similar way, you could say, "I have a blue ball." Or, you could say, "I have a bouncing ball."

The word "bouncing" serves the same purpose as the word "blue". They are both adjectives. But, "bouncing" can also be a verb. Don't get distracted; just look at the purposes the words serve!

Infinitives

As for infinitives, they are the most basic form of every verb. In English, they look like "to eat", "to sleep", "to hit", "to run". But, you would never "to eat" something.

I don't "to eat dinner". I eat dinner.

I don't "to sleep". I sleep.

In English, and most languages, we conjugate verbs when we use them. We don't use the raw infinitive.

But, we do use infinitives in other ways. For example, "I like to eat." In that case, "to eat" is the direct object of the verb "like". "To eat" is the thing that is liked.

We also sometimes say, "This is the guy to talk to." There, "to talk to" modifies "the guy". Infinitives can also be used to describe.

Finally, we can say, "I live to work." There, "to work" explains WHY I live, so it's an adverb.

The one thing infinitives cannot be is a verb. I know it seems weird, but that can actually help you remember it!

So, recap: Gerunds are nouns, never verbs. Participles are adjectives, never verbs. Infinitives can be anything but a verb. All of them LOOK like verbs, but they are never actual actions in any sentence.

Practice:

For practice, I want you to try to **find the actual verbs** through all the distractions! Then, you can **identify verb-like words and classify them** as Gerunds, Participles, or Infinitives.

1. To imitate Rita's singing would be unwise.
2. Cramming for the test is bad.
3. I opened the delivered package.
4. The man delivered a practiced speech.
5. To sleep twelve hours a day is difficult.
6. Fred mopped the vacuumed floor.
7. Paul loves running in the rain.
8. We came to cheer for the team.
9. Sarah hates cooked spinach.
10. John dislikes yelling.
11. To quit is to fail.
12. Singing in the rain is cliché.
13. Carlos is the counselor to talk to.
14. The fallen snow covered the mountain.
15. That was a moment to cherish.
16. Eating peaches wastes time that you need to keep.

Answers:

The verb
[other stuff]

1. [To imitate Rita's singing] **would be** unwise. (Infinitive phrase with a gerund inside it!)
2. [Cramming] for the test **is** bad. (Gerund)
3. I **opened** the [delivered] package. (Participle)
4. The man **delivered** a [practiced] speech. (Participle)
5. [To sleep twelve hours a day] **is** difficult. (Infinitive)
6. Fred **mopped** the [vacuumed] floor. (Participle)
7. Paul **loves** [running] in the rain. (Gerund, DO of "loves")
8. We **came** [to cheer] for the team. (Infinitive, adverb modifying "came")
9. Sarah **hates** [cooked] spinach. (Participle)
10. John **dislikes** [yelling]. (Gerund, Direct Object of "dislikes")
11. [To quit] **is** [to fail]. (both Infinitives)
12. [Singing] in the rain **is** cliché. (Gerund)
13. Carlos **is** the counselor [to talk to]. (Infinitive phrase, adjective modifying "counselor")
14. The [fallen] snow **covered** the mountain. (Participle)
15. That **was** a moment [to cherish]. (Infinitive, adjective modifying "moment")
16. [Eating] peaches **wastes** time that you need [to keep]. (Gerund, Subject. Infinitive, adverb modifying "need")

Selected Skills

Now we'll get into some of the core skills tested in the grammar section that are supported by all the stuff you've just learned. I'll pull questions from a few tests, but mostly from Test 1. So, we'll end up going through almost every Test 1 question by the end of the next couple chapters!

Subject Verb Agreement

This skill comes up a lot on SAT tests. Sometimes multiple times in one test. There are a few rules for this one.

Rule #1: DO NOT rely on "sound".

This skill will almost certainly sound weird to you. This is because, no matter what school you're in, they probably don't enforce grammar enough to get kids speaking correctly and properly all the time. So, unless your parents are Grammar professors who lecture you about grammar every day…this will sound weird. Your friends will all do this incorrectly, your teachers will probably also do this incorrectly (as they, themselves, are products of some school system which similarly dropped the ball on grammar). This is one of those rules that people get wrong, but you have to know how to do it right.

So, for this one, don't think about how it "sounds" or if it "sounds" right. None of that!

Rule #2: The subject of the sentence is NEVER inside of a prepositional phrase.

Each of the trainers **is** in the meeting.

This sentence is correct, though it might sound weird to you. The subject is "each". You should think of this as "each one". When you read it on the SAT, actually add the word "one" into the sentence in your head. It will help you remember that "each" is singular!

When we talk about each thing, we're talking about each thing separately, meaning singularly. This is important because you need to make the verb match the singular subject (or, if the question is asking for the subject, then you need to make the subject match).

So, "each one" IS something. You wouldn't say "each one ARE".

But, in true tricky SAT style, they include the prepositional phrase which has a **plural** noun in it, and that plural noun is the noun closest to the verb. So, you read:

Each of the **trainers is** in the meeting.

You see trainers (plural) and you think, Oh! It should be "are".

Now you know the trick; don't fall for it again!

Second example: None of the problems is wrong.

For the word "none", think of it as "not one". Actually do this on the SAT as well! The word "one" will remind you that "none" is also always singular.

"Not one IS". You wouldn't say, "Not one ARE".

The following indefinite pronouns are always singular:

another, anybody, anyone, anything, each, either, everybody, everyone, everything, little, much, neither, nobody, no one, none, nothing, one, other, somebody, someone, something

The following are always plural:

both, few, many, others, several

The following can be either singular OR plural:

all, any, more, most, some

You can say, "ALL of my arm is broken." (singular)

You can also say, "ALL of our friends are gone." (plural)

Practice:

Change the verb if it's wrong. If it's right, keep it.

1. Each of the students are tired.
2. All of my friends are from New York.
3. None of the cups are full.
4. Most of my things is missing.
5. Each of the dogs like running.
6. All of my head hurts.
7. All of the attendees are present.
8. One of my friends live in a box.
9. Running several businesses are challenging.
10. Eating three meals is fun.

Answers:

1. Each ONE of the students **IS** tired.
2. All of my friends are from New York. (Correct)
3. NOT ONE of the cups **IS** full.
4. Most of my things **ARE** missing.
5. Each ONE of the dogs **LIKES** running.
6. All of my head hurts. (Correct)
7. All of the attendees are present. (Correct)
8. ONE of my friends **LIVES** in a box.
9. Running several businesses **IS** challenging. The subject is "running. So, you can think of it this way: Running is challenging.
10. Eating three meals is fun. (Correct) Same idea: Eating is fun.

Rule #3 for Subject Verb Agreement: Compound subjects are plural.

This one is simpler, and most students don't get it wrong. But, still be aware of it.

John and Paul **like** to swim in the lake. ("John and Paul" is a plural subject.)

However, if the subject contains "or" or "nor", then you match up the verb with the noun closest to the verb.

Either Fred or the other members of the band **have** to take this home. (We match up "have" with the plural "members of the band".)

Practice:

Change the verb if it's wrong. If it's right, keep it.

1. John and Paul, the founders of the club, is not here.
2. Bob and Simon, who love to travel extensively in the far east, thinks it's best if we travel by car.
3. On the program is a speech and a song.
4. There is a Frisbee and a book in the lake.
5. Neither the secretaries nor the president are available.
6. Fred or his father is in the room.
7. On the program is a violin solo and a dance.
8. In the boat is a policeman and a sailor.
9. On the menu is a hamburger or a steak.

Answers:

1. John and Paul, the founders of the club, **ARE** not here.

2. Bob and Simon, who love to travel extensively in the far east, **THINK** it's best if we travel by car.

3. On the program **ARE** a speech and a song.

4. There **ARE** a Frisbee and a book in the lake.

5. Neither the secretaries nor the president **IS** available.

6. Fred or his father is in the room. (Correct)

7. On the program **ARE** a violin solo and a dance.

8. In the boat **ARE** a policeman and a sailor.

9. On the menu is a hamburger or a steak. (Correct)

Harder Practice:

Find the subject of the bolded verb, then correct the verb if necessary.

1. The share of library materials that is in nonprint formats **are** increasing steadily.

2. According to Dr. Box, a leading Greenland expert, tundra fires in 2012 from as far away as North America produced great amounts of soot, some of which drifted over Greenland in giant plumes of smoke and then **fell** as particles onto the ice sheet.

3. Because philosophy **teaching** students not what to think but how to think, the age-old discipline offers consistently useful tools for academic and professional achievement.

4. On the Graduate Record Examination (GRE), for example, students intending to study philosophy in graduate school **has scored** higher than students in all but four other majors.

5. Employment in all job sectors in the United States is projected to grow by fourteen percent over the next decade, yet the expected growth rate for librarians is predicted to be only seven percent, or half of the overall rate. This trend, combined with the increasing accessibility of information via the Internet, **have** led some to claim that librarianship is in decline as a profession. As public libraries adapt to rapid technological advances in information distribution, librarians' roles are actually expanding.

6. As a result, organic material that is sent to landfills ★ **contribute** ★ to the release of methane, a very potent greenhouse gas.

7. Yet some of the earliest known works of art, including paintings and drawings tens of thousands of years old found on cave walls in Spain and France, ★ **portrays** ★ animals.

8. This deformation results in subtle variations in density that both ★ **causes uneven heat flow and limits** ★ the size of the droplets that can be tested.

9. According to Box, a leading Greenland expert, tundra fires in 2012 from as far away as North America produced great amounts of soot, some of which drifted over Greenland in giant plumes of smoke and then ★ **had fallen** ★ as particles onto the ice sheet.

Answers:

SUBJECT
CORRECTED VERB
[other things of note!]

1. The SHARE [of library materials] (prep phrase, cannot contain subject) [that is in nonprint formats] (adj clause, cannot contain main subject) ✷ **IS** ✷ increasing steadily. ("share" is singular.)

2. According to Dr. Box, a leading Greenland expert, tundra FIRES in 2012 [from as far away as North America] (prep phrase) **produced** (this matches fires, the main subject) great amounts of soot, [SOME of which **drifted** (matches "some") over Greenland in giant plumes of smoke and then ✷ **fell** ✷ (matches "some") as particles onto the ice sheet]. (one big adj clause modifying "soot")

3. [Because PHILOSOPHY ✷ **teaches** ✷ (this is more of a conjugation issue) students not what to think but how to think] (adv clause modifying "offers"), the age-old discipline offers consistently useful tools for academic and professional achievement.

4. On the Graduate Record Examination (GRE), for example, STUDENTS [intending [to study philosophy] [in graduate school]] (participle phrase with an infinitive and a prep phrase inside) ✷ **have scored** ✷ ("students" is plural, "has scored" was singular. Had to change it.) higher than students in all but four other majors.

5. Employment in all job sectors in the United States is projected to grow by fourteen percent over the next decade, yet the expected growth rate for librarians is predicted to be only seven percent, or half of the overall rate. This TREND, [combined with the increasing accessibility of information via the Internet] (participle phrase with several prep phrases inside), ★ **has** ★ ("trend" is singular, "have" was plural) led some to claim that librarianship is in decline as a profession. As public libraries adapt to rapid technological advances in information distribution, librarians' roles are actually expanding.

6. As a result, organic MATERIAL [that is sent to landfills] (adj clause modifying material) ★ **contributes** ★ ("material" is singular, "contribute" was plural) to the release of methane, a very potent greenhouse gas.

7. Yet SOME [of the earliest known works] [of art] (prep phrases), [including paintings and drawings tens of thousands of years old found on cave walls in Spain and France], (participle phrase with stuff in it) ★ **portrays** ★ animals. (Correct)

8. This deformation results in subtle variations in density [that both ☆ **causes uneven heat flow and limits** ☆ the size of the droplets] (adjective clause) that can be tested.

First, figure out what that adjective clause is modifying!

Then, recognize that the word "that" inside of the adj clause will be referring to whatever the clause modifies. Therefore, "that" will have the same quantity. If the modified word is singular, then "that" will be singular. If the modified word is plural, then "that" will be plural.

So, what does the clause modify? "Variations".

Variations is plural, therefore the verbs in the clause should also be plural.

This deformation results in subtle variations in density [that both ☆ **cause uneven heat flow and limit** ☆ the size of the droplets] that can be tested.

9. According to Box, a leading Greenland expert, tundra fires in 2012 from as far away as North America produced great amounts of soot, some of which drifted over Greenland in giant plumes of smoke and then ☆ **had fallen** ☆ as particles onto the ice sheet.

This verb is also inside of a modifying clause. So, figure out what the adjective clause is modifying, then make the verb match that word.

ALSO, we need all verbs inside of this one clause to match. This is always true for compound verbs. Compound verbs are only separated by the word "and", meaning they are both the main verbs of the clause. Verbs in separate clauses don't have to match (though they often do, or there is some logic to the flow of tenses). But compound verbs do need to match.

You might say, "I sang and danced." You would not say, "I sang and am dancing." To show a progression of events, you could say, "I sang, and now I am dancing." That has two separate clauses, and it shows a transition of time.

So! The other verb in this clause is "drifted" which is simple past tense. The noun being modified is "great amounts of soot" which is plural. And the subject of the adjective clause is "some" which refers to those great amounts of soot.

According to Box, a leading Greenland expert, tundra fires in 2012 from as far away as North America produced great amounts of soot, some of which drifted over Greenland in giant plumes of smoke and then ☆ **fell** ☆ as particles onto the ice sheet.

Dangling Modifiers

This skill is maybe 1 or 2 questions per SAT. Every question counts! And this skill is pretty easy once you get it.

The rule is, if there's an adjective phrase in the front of any sentence, it must be modifying the very first word in that sentence (in other words, the word that the phrase is touching).

Wrong: Developed by an experienced staff, **the President** introduced his plan today.

It wasn't the president who was "developed by an experienced staff". The plan was.

So, it should read like this:

Correct: Developed by an experienced staff, the plan was introduced by the president today.

The "plan" is directly next to the phrase that modifies it.

Practice Level 1:

Rearrange the sentence, if necessary, so that the intro phrase is closest to the word it modifies.

1. Sitting quietly, Fred's ears caught the sound of a rat.
2. Jumping up and down, the shipwrecked people caught the ship's attention.
3. Stepping silently, the King's cat walked home.
4. Running through the stream, the deer's eyes noticed the hunters.
5. Flying in circles around my room and crashing into windows, I was annoyed by the bee.

Answers:

1. Sitting quietly, **Fred** caught the sound of a rat. ("Fred's ears" didn't catch anything.)

2. Jumping up and down, the shipwrecked people caught the ship's attention. (Correct)

3. Stepping silently, the King's cat walked home. (Correct)

4. Running through the stream, the **deer** noticed the hunters. (the "deer's eyes" weren't running anywhere…)

5. Flying in circles around my room and crashing into windows, the bee annoyed me. ("I" wasn't flying in circles and crashing into windows.)

Practice Level 2:

1. ☆ **Dotted with pin-sized knobs, another visitor noticed my fascination with a tiny writing desk and its drawers.** ☆

    Correct the sentence above.

    (A) NO CHANGE
    (B) Another visitor, dotted with pin-sized knobs, noticed my fascination with a tiny writing desk and its drawers.
    (C) Another visitor dotted with pin-sized knobs noticed my fascination with a tiny writing desk and its drawers.
    (D) Another visitor noticed my fascination with a tiny writing desk and its drawers, dotted with pin-sized knobs.

2. Within a month, I found myself feeling isolated despite having frequent email and instant messaging contact with my colleagues. Having become frustrated trying to solve difficult problems, ☆ **no colleagues were nearby to share ideas.** ☆ It was during this time that I read an article about coworking spaces.

    (A) NO CHANGE
    (B) colleagues were important for sharing ideas.
    (C) ideas couldn't be shared with colleagues.
    (D) I missed having colleagues nearby to consult.

3. Approaching a doorway in which dangles a red envelope filled with green paper money, the ★ **lion's teeth snare the envelope.** ★

    (A) NO CHANGE
    (B) lion snares the envelope with its teeth.
    (C) envelope is snared by the lion with its teeth.
    (D) teeth of the lion snare the envelope.

4. Here's a curveball of a question!

    A group of engineering students from the University of California at San Diego (UCSD), for example, ★ **tried to find a method to make their biofuel combustion study** ★ (fuels derived from once-living material) free of the drawbacks researchers face on Earth.

    (A) NO CHANGE
    (B) strove for a method to make their study of biofuel combustion
    (C) sought a method to study combustion of biofuels
    (D) looked for a method to study biofuel combustion

Answers:

1 is D.

2 is D.

3 is B.

4 is C.

4 was the hardest of those. The bolded bit is modified by the bit in parentheses. The bit in parentheses talks about "fuels", but the word closest to "fuels" is "study". The study isn't a type of plural fuels. But, if we change it to C, then the last word is "biofuels", and biofuels are, indeed, fuels derived from once-living material.

Pronoun-Antecedent Agreement

This skill also comes up around 1-3 times per test. You're likely to see it, and it's easier than subject-verb agreement!

Pronouns represent other things.

Pronoun examples: "he, she, it/its, they, we, me, them, our/ours, their/theirs"

The only thing that matters here is that you know what the pronoun is referring to. The SAT will create questions where the pronoun and the word it refers to won't match.

Something like this:

Fred is tall. They like basketball.

Fred is singular; he's not a "they". "They" is plural (based on the formal rules of grammar).

Most of the time, these questions won't involve people. They'll refer to other nouns like this:

For years, for a lifetime, the machinery of my destiny has worked in secret to prepare for this moment; **their** clockwork has moved exactly toward this time and place and no other.

The pronoun "their" refers to the subject of the previous sentence: "machinery". "Machinery" is singular; "their" is plural. You would need to change "their" to "its", a singular possessive.

What makes these questions hard is that usually the antecedent and the pronoun will be separated by a lot of prepositional phrases, various clauses, etc. That means there will be several nouns, and you need to pick out the correct antecedent that attaches to the pronoun in question.

Practice:

1. Scientists have long known that soot particles facilitate melting by darkening snow and ice, limiting ★ **its** ★ ability to reflect the Sun's rays.

2. As the parade winds its way through Chinatown, the music crescendos, and the lion dance reaches ★ **their** ★ climax with the "plucking of the greens."

3. Because today's students can expect to hold multiple jobs—some of which may not even exist yet—during ★ **our** ★ lifetime, studying philosophy allows them to be flexible and adaptable.

4. A recent study by two professors at the University of California, Santa Cruz, Chris Wilmers and James Estes, suggests that kelp forests protected by sea otters can absorb as much as twelve times the amount of carbon dioxide from the atmosphere as those where sea urchins are allowed to devour the kelp. Like its terrestrial plant cousins, kelp removes carbon dioxide from the atmosphere, turning it into sugar fuel through photosynthesis, and releases oxygen back into the air. Scientists knew this but did not recognize ★ **how large a role they played** ★ in helping kelp forests to significantly decrease the amount of carbon dioxide in the atmosphere.

   (A) NO CHANGE
   (B) how large a role that it played
   (C) how large a role sea otters played
   (D) that they played such a large role

Answers:

1. Scientists (main subject) **have long known** (main verb) [that soot PARTICLES (noun clause's subject) **facilitate** (noun clause's verb) melting (gerund and DO) by darkening snow and ice, limiting ⋆ **their** ⋆ ability to reflect the Sun's rays] (one big noun clause acting as the DO!)

   This one is correct. If you got a little confused with it, just think about what thing(s) would be doing the reflecting of the Sun's rays. It wouldn't be the soot particles; it would be the snow and ice. You've seen snow and ice before on a sunny day (probably). It's very bright. So, don't just rely on rules! Also use logic.

2. As the parade winds its way through Chinatown, the music crescendos, and the lion dance reaches ⋆ **their** ⋆ climax with the "plucking of the greens."

3. Because today's students can expect to hold multiple jobs—some of which may not even exist yet—during ⋆ **our** ⋆ lifetime, studying philosophy allows them to be flexible and adaptable.

4. Answer is C. This one is a fun challenge.

The issue here is that the noun is nowhere near the pronoun! You have to just use logic to figure out what "they" is supposed to be referring to. And THEN, you have to recognize that you can't just go around referring to stuff with pronouns if you haven't talked about that stuff recently.

I can't say, "Bob is a really cool guy. Sometimes it rains in our town, and when it does, there's often flooding. The flooding can be pretty severe. Once, an entire street had to be replaced. He likes climbing."

By the time you get to "he likes climbing", you've forgotten about Bob. That's exactly what happened with the sea otters here.

Possessive vs Plural

Plural nouns show more than one thing. Possessives show that you are owning or possessing something. Sounds simple, but you have to pay attention because the questions will often be tricky (big surprise, I know).

One extra bit:

Singular nouns can possess things. As in, "The dog's toy is in the yard."

But also! Plural nouns can possess things. As in, "Our dogs' play date is tomorrow." All of the dogs collectively have the play date.

Also, "I have two sisters. My sisters' mom is also my mom."

Whenever the noun is plural, you put the apostrophe at the end. When it's singular, you do [apostrophe S].

Easier Practice First:

Fill in the blanks with either plural or possessive.

1. The _____ egg hatched. (eagle)
2. The airplane was three _____ late. (hour)
3. My _____ tire was flat. (bicycle)
4. Did you go to _____ house last night? (Evan)
5. The _____ anchor weighed fifty pounds. (boat)

Add apostrophes as needed or mark the sentence "correct".

6. The mens horses were near the lake.
7. The tourists' photographs were compiled on the website.
8. The wind blew the flowers petals away.
9. I like the style of these headphones.
10. I like all these headphones styles.
11. All the elephants' trunks were four feet long.

Answers:

1. The eagle's egg hatched. (possessive)
2. The airplane was three hours late. (plural)
3. My bicycle's tire was flat. (possessive)
4. Did you go to Evan's house last night? (possessive)
5. The boat's anchor weighed fifty pounds. (possessive)

6. The **mens'** horses were near the lake.
7. The tourists' photographs were compiled on the website. **Correct**
8. The wind blew the **flower's** petals away.
9. I like the style of these headphones. **Correct**
10. I like all these **headphones'** styles.
11. All the elephants' trunks were four feet long. **Correct**

Harder Practice:

1. As I walked through the exhibit, I overheard a **visitors' remark,** "You know, that grandfather clock actually runs. Its glass door swings open, and the clock can be wound up."

    (A) NO CHANGE
    (B) visitors remarking,
    (C) visitor remarked,
    (D) visitor remark,

2. If it is improperly introduced into the environment, acid-whey runoff **can pollute waterways,** depleting the oxygen content of streams and rivers as it decomposes.

    (A) NO CHANGE
    (B) can pollute waterway's,
    (C) could have polluted waterways,
    (D) has polluted waterways,

3. These days, many **student's majoring** in philosophy have no intention of becoming philosophers; instead they plan to apply those skills to other disciplines.

    Explain what's wrong with the bolded portion above.

Answers:

1. Answer is D. This one isn't a possessive. It's more like saying:
   ...and then Fred said, "blah blah blah".
   That's how we introduce what people say.

2. Answer is A. This one is just plural.

3. There is no student possessing anything. It's just a bunch of students who are majoring in philosophy. So, it should be "students".

Faulty Parallelism

In general, in English, we like for things to match.

Fred likes running, jumping, and to swim. (This, we don't like.)

Fred likes running, jumping, and swimming. (This, we like.)

That's all!

Practice:

If anything doesn't fit, replace it with something that would match.

1. Fred is taking science, math, and Political Science 101.

2. Fred went to swim, to run, and to the store.

3. Yesterday Fred went to the park, ate a sandwich, bought a boat, and a car.

4. Sonia is known for her independence, honesty, and being intelligent.

5. The dancer was praised not only for her strength but also in her agility.

6. To complete the music program, a student must present one vocal performance, one instrumental performance, and composing one original work.

7. Studies have suggested that eating nuts—almonds in particular—might help to lower blood cholesterol levels in humans and reducing the risk of heart disease by protecting the blood vessels.

8. Because I was hungry, tired, and feeling like I was sad, I did not want to go to my appointment.

9. Stand-up comedy, one of the least respected performing arts, is valuable to society because the performer is able to inform the audience and making it laugh uncontrollably.

10. Exercising enabled Joe to strengthen his muscles and releasing his stress.

11. Librarians must now be proficient curators of electronic information, compiling, **catalog,** and updating these collections.

    (A) NO CHANGE
    (B) librarians cataloging,
    (C) to catalog,
    (D) cataloging,

12. The room is simple but spacious, with a small sink and counter along one wall, a cast-iron wood stove and some hanging pots and pans against another wall, and **a small table under a window of the third wall.** Aside from a few simple wooden chairs placed near the edges of the room, the floor is open and obviously well worn.

    Which choice most closely matches the stylistic pattern established earlier in the sentence?

    (A) NO CHANGE
    (B) a small table is under the third wall's window.
    (C) the third wall has a window and small table.
    (D) the third wall has a small table against it and a window.

13. Studies have shown that employees are happier, **healthier, and more** productive when they work in an environment that affords them adequate amounts of natural light.

    Explain why the following answer choice can't be right.

    (B) health, and more

14. Nutritionists consider Greek yogurt to be a healthy food: it is an excellent source of calcium and protein, serves as a digestive aid, and ☆ **it contains** ☆ few calories in its unsweetened low- and non-fat forms.

   (A) NO CHANGE
   (B) containing
   (C) contains
   (D) will contain

Answers:

1. Fred is taking science, math, and **history (or some other generic topic).**

2. Fred went to swim, to run, and **to bike (or some other infinitive).**

3. Yesterday Fred ate a sandwich, bought a boat, and **drove a car (or did some other thing with the car).**

4. Sonia is known for her independence, honesty, and **intelligence**.

5. The dancer was praised not only for her strength but also **(take out the word "in")** her agility.

6. To complete the music program, a student must present one vocal performance, one instrumental performance, and **(take out "composing")** one original work.

7. Studies have suggested that eating nuts—almonds in particular—might help to lower blood cholesterol levels in humans and **reduce (matches the structure of the verb "lower")** the risk of heart disease by protecting the blood vessels. (Note: "to lower" is an infinitive. To find a matching verb structure, try adding "to" in front. You want something that is essentially an infinitive, but the word "to" was already said with the first infinitive.)

8. Because I was hungry, tired, and **sad (sad matches the others)**, I did not want to go to my appointment.

9. Stand-up comedy, one of the least respected performing arts, is valuable to society because the performer is able to inform the audience and **make (matches the structure of "inform")** it laugh uncontrollably. (Note: Again, "to inform" is an infinitive.

"to make" would also be an infinitive. "to making" is not an infinitive.)

10. Exercising enabled Joe to strengthen his muscles and **release (matches "strengthen")** his stress.

11. Answer is C. Parallel structure.

12. Answer is A. For C and D, the rest would be phrased as "the first wall has…and the second wall has…and then either C or D."

    The issue with B is that it suddenly includes a verb. The other pieces don't have verbs in them.

13. "healthier" matches "happier". "health" wouldn't match.

14. Answer is C. The issue here is that you only need to say "it" once. It is an excellent source of calcium and protein, IT serves as a digestive aid, and IT contains few calories… You could put all of the "ITS" in there, or you can just keep the first one. But, you can't keep the first and the last, and not the one in the middle.

Redundancy

This one is pretty common. It comes up a few times per test.

WRONG: Eventually, I hope to make a lot of money **in the long run.**

RIGHT: Eventually, I hope to make a lot of money.

RIGHT: I hope to make a lot of money **in the long run.**

"Eventually" and "in the long run" mean the same thing. Thus, you don't need both. In other words, having both is redundant.

The way that this skill gets tough is that the sentences get…you guessed it…super long. So, the two bits that might be redundant might also be pretty far away from each other. Hence the whole reading carefully thing, you know.

Practice:

Fix each of the following sentences. If the sentence is correct, write "correct."

1. This unique, one-of-a-kind vase is modestly priced at $100.
2. Fred plans to go to law school eventually.
3. Fred found an unusually large turtle that was bigger than an average turtle.
4. The paper was unusual and different from the norm.
5. The verbose, wordy paper contained a lot of extra words.
6. The tall, furious giraffe attacked the tourists.
7. The State Department does an annual report each year that looks at expenses and security.
8. Every year, they hold an annual celebration of the yearly anniversary.
9. In fact, librarians' training now includes courses on research and Internet search methods; many librarians teach classes in Internet navigation, database and software use, and digital information literacy is taught by them.
10. Free to all who utilize their services, public libraries and librarians are especially valuable, because they offer free resources that may be difficult to find elsewhere, such as help with online job searches as well as résumé and job material development.

11. When it comes to the free services libraries provide, public libraries and librarians are especially valuable, because they offer free resources that may be difficult to find elsewhere, such as help with online job searches as well as résumé and job material development.

12. The pattern Box observed in 2012 may repeat itself again, with harmful effects on the Arctic ecosystem.

13. The novelty of this comfortable work-from-home life, however, soon got worn off quickly.

14. To address the problem of disposal, farmers have found a number of uses for acid whey. They can add it to livestock feed as a protein supplement, which provides an important element of their diet.

15. Typically, the ice sheet begins to show evidence of thawing in late **summer. This follows** several weeks of higher temperatures.

    NOTE: Recognize that there is nothing wrong with the sentence as is. Yet, "no change" isn't even an option. Why? Because they want it to be more succinct. This thought doesn't need to be two sentences. *It also doesn't need to be one, clunky sentence!!* This does tie a bit into the skill of Brevity, also.

    Which choice most effectively combines the two sentences at the italicized portion?

    (A) summer, following
    (B) summer, and this thawing follows
    (C) summer, and such thawing follows
    (D) summer and this evidence follows

Answers:

1. This unique vase is modestly priced at $100. **(You could keep one or the other, not both.)**

2. Fred plans to go to law school. **(If you have a plan, then you don't need to say "eventually". All plans are in the future. OR, you could take out "plan".)**

3. Fred found an unusually large turtle. **(Or you could take out "unusually large".)**

4. The paper was unusual. **(Or you could take out "unusual".)**

5. The paper was verbose. **(Or you could keep any of the other instances of the same word.)**

6. The tall, furious giraffe attacked the tourists. **(Correct)**

7. The State Department does an annual report that looks at expenses and security. **(Take out "each year" or take out "annual".)**

8. Every year, they hold a celebration. **(Or take out one of the other bits that meant "yearly".)**

9. In fact, librarians' training now includes courses on research and Internet search methods; many librarians **[teach classes]** in Internet navigation, database and software use, and digital information literacy is **[taught by them]**. (Those two pieces are redundant.)

10. **[Free to all who utilize their services]**, public libraries and librarians are especially valuable, because they offer **[free resources]** that may be difficult to find elsewhere, such as help with online job searches as well as résumé and job material development. (Those two pieces are redundant.)

11. [**When it comes to the free services libraries provide**], public libraries and librarians are especially valuable, because they offer [**free resources**] that may be difficult to find elsewhere, such as help with online job searches as well as résumé and job material development. (Those two pieces are redundant.)

12. The pattern Box observed in 2012 may [**repeat**] itself [**again**], with harmful effects on the Arctic ecosystem. (Those two pieces are redundant.)

13. The novelty of this comfortable work-from-home life, however, [**soon**] got worn off [**quickly**]. (Those two pieces are redundant.)

14. To address the problem of disposal, farmers have found a number of uses for acid whey. They can add it to livestock feed as a [**protein supplement**], [**which provides an important element of their diet**]. (We already know that a protein supplement would be an important element of their diet.)

15. Answer is A. This one also ties in with Brevity. It makes things shorter and simpler.

Brevity

The idea here is that if you can say something in 5 words instead of 50, you should do that. (I know, it's very ironic since the reading passages are full of 50+ word sentences...)

How will the SAT try to trick you? They'll make the shortest answer also include some grammatical mistake. Wrong punctuation, bad subject verb agreement, no independent clauses, something like that.

So, don't just pick the shortest answer. Look for other grammatical errors to disprove answer choices, then pick the shortest, grammatically correct sentence.

Practice:

1. In broad terms, philosophy is the study of meaning and the values underlying thought and behavior. But **more pragmatically,** the discipline encourages students to analyze complex material, question conventional beliefs, and express thoughts in a concise manner.

    (A) NO CHANGE
    (B) speaking in a more pragmatic way,
    (C) speaking in a way more pragmatically,
    (D) in a more pragmatic-speaking way,

2. Studies have found that those students who major in philosophy often do better than students from other majors in both verbal reasoning and analytical **writing. These results can be** measured by standardized test scores.

    (A) writing as
    (B) writing, and these results can be
    (C) writing, which can also be
    (D) writing when the results are

Answers:

1. Answer is A. That's the simplest and shortest.

2. Answer is also A. Combining the sentences makes it shorter and simpler.

Here's an interesting instance of brevity:

I like walking my dog; I also like running with him.

You could say the above, and it's grammatically correct. But it could still be more succinct!

More Practice:

If the sentence can be made more succinct, then rewrite it! Otherwise, write "Correct".

1. The books were old and worn; they were covered in dust.
2. The tree was shedding its leaves for the winter.
3. The floor shook. It was shaking during the earthquake.
4. The teacups had delicate handles. They had floral patterns painted on them.
5. The couch and chairs, in keeping with the style of the time, are characterized by elegantly curved arms and ★ **legs, they** ★ are covered in luxurious velvet.

    (A) NO CHANGE
    (B) legs, the couch and chairs
    (C) legs and
    (D) legs,

6. The crowd has gathered to celebrate Lunar New Year. The street is a sea of ★ **red. Red is** ★ the traditional Chinese color of luck and happiness.

    (A) red,
    (B) red; in addition, red is
    (C) red; in other words, red is
    (D) red, the color; that is

7. Approaching a doorway in which dangles a red envelope filled with green paper money, the lion snares the envelope with its teeth. It then chews up the bills and spits out the ☆ **money-filled envelope instead of chewing it up.** ☆

   (A) NO CHANGE
   (B) envelope that had been dangling from the doorway.
   (C) envelope that had the money in it.
   (D) envelope.

8. However, with the rise of high-quality recording technology, reliance on court reporters **each as record keepers** is decreasing.

   Explain why the bolded portion above is wrong.

9. Champions of court reporting, though, argue the ☆ **opposite. They argue** ☆ that with the increased reliance on technology, errors actually increase. Because digital systems record indiscriminately, they cannot discern important parts of the proceedings from other noises in the courtroom. In other words, a digital device does indeed record everything, but that includes loud noises, such as a book dropping, that can make the actual words spoken impossible to hear.

   Which choice most effectively combines the sentences at the underlined portion?

   (A) opposite, such
   (B) opposite—
   (C) opposite, which is
   (D) opposite; their opinion is

Answers:

1. The books were old, worn, and covered in dust.

   (Note: This isn't exactly parallel structure, but sometimes we make an exception and allow the very last thing to be **slightly** different. However, "covered in dust" is still a simple, physical description, just like "old" and "worn". Also, this is only for the last one. We wouldn't say:

   The books were covered in dust, old, and worn.

   And we also wouldn't say:

   The books were old, covered in dust, and worn.)

2. The tree was shedding its leaves for the winter. **Correct**

3. The floor shook during the earthquake.

4. The teacups had delicate handles with floral patterns painted on them.

5. C

6. A

7. D (This one also ties in Redundancy!)

8. That part isn't necessary. We're already talking about record keeping; that's what court reporters do.

9. B (You'll learn more about hyphens later.)

Faulty Comparisons

This is another one that general people in the world constantly get wrong. So, it won't "sound" wrong to you necessarily. But, don't be dumb! We do not do the Grammar section based on how things "sound"!!

Incorrect: Fred's car is faster than Joe.

The speaker is trying to say that Fred's car is faster than Joe's car. What he is actually saying is that Fred's car can travel faster than Joe can run. That's silly.

Correct: Fred's car can travel faster than Joe's car.

OR

Correct: Fred's car can travel faster than Joe's.

Practice:

Fix the following sentences, if necessary. If the sentence is fine, leave it blank.

1. American cars are much faster than England.

2. The sandwiches at Panera cost more than Cosi.

3. Fred's shoes are better quality than those at the department store.

4. Zoe's dress is more costly than Sarah's.

5. The computers made today are much faster than the twentieth century.

6. The lion dance requires the strength, grace, and coordination of two dancers. Many of the moves in the dance, such as jumps, rolls, and kicks, are similar to **martial arts and acrobatics.**

    (A) NO CHANGE
    (B) the disciplines of martial arts and acrobatics.
    (C) martial artists and acrobats.
    (D) those in martial arts and acrobatics.

Answers: (There are a few ways you can do these. The following are acceptable options.)

1. American cars are much faster than English cars.

2. The sandwiches at Panera cost more than Cosi's.
   The sandwiches at Panera cost more than those at Cosi.

3. Fred's shoes are better quality than those at the department store. **(Correct)**

4. Zoe's dress is more costly than Sarah's. **(Correct)**

5. The computers made today are much faster than those of the twentieth century.

6. Answer is D.

Punctuation Skills

Commas

Sometimes modifiers are separated from whatever they modify by commas. But, how do we know if we need commas or not?

You take out whatever is inside the commas and see if the sentence still makes sense. This is pretty common with commas. You always want to look at the sentence without the extra info, see if it makes sense, and then use commas or not accordingly.

I couldn't wait to see painter, Georges Seurat's, famous painting.

Without the information in the commas, it reads:

I couldn't wait to see painter famous painting.

Since that doesn't make any sense at all, you know that you NEED the information "Georges Seurat's".

Since you NEED the information, you canNOT have any commas. The corrected sentence would read:

I couldn't wait to see painter Georges Seurat's famous painting.

Whenever you need the information, you cannot have commas. The idea is that commas indicate less important information, modifying information, information that isn't crucial to the functioning of the sentence. You would never use commas to set off the verb or the subject. Those things are important! Similarly, anything that is important or necessary to the sentence should stand out, not be surrounded by commas.

Note that commas are also used for other things like separating a Dependent Clause from an Independent Clause, setting apart various types of phrases, or separating items in a list. Those are separate rules. Here, we're really talking about the use of commas to set apart some modifying information.

Second Example: I couldn't wait to see Georges Seurat's famous painting, *A Sunday Afternoon on the Island of La Grande Jatte.*

Notice that in the above, the information to the right of the comma is not NEEDED. That's why you keep that comma in there.

Practice:

The extra information is shown in brackets. Decide if the extra information should be separated by commas or not. If so, add them in.

1. I invited Fred [the new student in our class] to come to the party.
2. Mom will make my favorite meal [spaghetti] for my birthday.
3. Students [who break the honor code] are expelled.
4. Paul's wife [Clara] is president of the local Red Cross.
5. The German writer [Hermann Hesse] is a favorite with American college students.
6. The cake was made for our nephew [Carlton's] birthday.
7. Bob [the kid in the baseball cap] is my new friend.
8. Our teacher [Mr. Fred] gave us no homework tonight.
9. I was excited to taste owner [Margot Lilly's] new tea blend.

Answers:

1. I invited Fred, the new student in our class, to come to the party. (Commas)

2. Mom will make my favorite meal, spaghetti, for my birthday. (Commas)

3. Students who break the honor code are expelled. (No Commas)

4. Paul's wife, Clara, is president of the local Red Cross. (Commas)

5. The German writer Hermann Hesse is a favorite with American college students. (No Commas)

6. The cake was made for our nephew Carlton's birthday. (No Commas)

7. Bob, the kid in the baseball cap, is my new friend. (Commas)

8. Our teacher, Mr. Fred, gave us no homework tonight. (Commas)

9. I was excited to taste owner Margot Lilly's new tea blend. (No Commas)

Sometimes, the extra information is just another way of saying the original thing. Like, a word and then its definition or explanation.

The exchange rate for the Pound, **the currency of Britain**, went up.

The pound IS the currency of Britain. So, this is just redefining for anyone who doesn't know.

This skill goes one step further. Sometimes we use these appositives to describe people or things; you've seen that already. But **sometimes** we use them to describe vague people like "the man" or "the woman". For that, we have a slightly altered rule.

Correct: The man saw a tree.
Also Correct: The man who lives nearby saw a tree. (no commas)

Although the sentence DOES make sense without the added information, we still consider it "necessary" because we just don't know who this man is. Extra information about him is highly desirable.

Correct: Fred saw the man **who won the gold medal**.
Also Correct: Fred studied Abraham Lincoln, **who was the sixteenth president**.

In the first sentence, we don't know WHICH man Fred saw. That added information is very helpful to us. So, it doesn't get a comma.

In the second sentence, we already know who Abraham Lincoln is, so that added information isn't as useful. Therefore, it does get a comma.

Necessary info = NO commas
Unnecessary info = surrounded by commas

For these comma rules, you may need to read this section several times on different days. Grammar takes time to internalize. It doesn't take a lot of time to **understand** because it's just made up rules. Reading has some understanding and comprehension. Math has some logical and puzzle solving. Grammar is pretty much just rules. BUT, you can't just read them once and know them forever.

When I finally learned how to use Who vs Whom in a sentence, it took me a solid month or two to get perfectly, consistently good with it. I knew the rule, but I still had to think it out slowly each time. Now, though, I can correct other people's bad grammar the second I hear it come out of their mouths. That's what true mastery for Grammar looks like!

So, don't be afraid to read and reread and re-re-reread. You're not stupid or slow or a bad learner. You're just learnING. It's a process.

Practice:

Decide if the extra information should be separated by commas or not. If so, add them in.

1. John [whom I met yesterday] shot a deer that was running away.
2. When I was six, Gerald [whom I feared] gave me some gum.
3. The man [who lives in Mexico] saw Barack Obama [who made a speech yesterday].
4. The salesman [who showed me this radio] is not here right now.
5. Eric Hubert [who showed me this radio] is not here right now.
6. Did you know that James Agee [the novelist and poet] was also a film critic?
7. The guy [who ate the last cookie] hopes to graduate from law school.
8. The woman [who worked in the dress shop] hoped to see the play.
9. They suggest that the presence of otters provides a good model of how carbon can be sequestered, **or removed; from** the atmosphere through the management of animal populations.

    (A) NO CHANGE
    (B) or removed from,
    (C) or, removed from,
    (D) or removed, from

10. Planned obsolescence, a practice whereby products are designed to have a limited period of ☆ **usefulness,** ☆ has been a cornerstone of manufacturing strategy for the past 80 years.

(A) NO CHANGE
(B) usefulness—
(C) usefulness;
(D) usefulness

11. The summer of 2012 was the warmest in 170 years, records show. But Jason ☆ **Box, an associate professor of geology at Ohio State** ☆ believes that another factor added to the early thaw: the "dark snow" problem.

(A) NO CHANGE
(B) Box an associate professor of geology at Ohio State,
(C) Box, an associate professor of geology at Ohio State,
(D) Box, an associate professor of geology, at Ohio State

12. On the plane's ascent, passengers feel twice Earth's gravitational pull, but for brief periods at the peak of the trajectory, ☆ **"weightlessness" or microgravity similar to what is experienced in space,** ☆ is achieved.

(A) NO CHANGE
(B) "weightlessness" or microgravity, similar to what is experienced, in space
(C) "weightlessness" or, microgravity, similar to what is experienced in space
(D) "weightlessness," or microgravity similar to what is experienced in space,

Answers:

1. John, whom I met yesterday, shot a deer that was running away.
2. When I was six, Gerald, whom I feared, gave me some gum.
3. The man who lives in Mexico saw Barack Obama, who made a speech yesterday. (No commas for the first clause. Commas for the second.)
4. The salesman who showed me this radio is not here right now. (No commas)
5. Eric Hubert, who showed me this radio, is not here right now.
6. Did you know that James Agee, the novelist and poet, was also a film critic?
7. The guy who ate the last cookie hopes to graduate from law school. (No commas)
8. The woman who worked in the dress shop hoped to see the play. (No commas)
9. Answer is D.

    They suggest that the presence of otters provides a good model of how carbon can be sequestered, or removed, from the atmosphere through the management of animal populations.

    This is a simple restating of the same thing.

10. Answer is A.

    Planned obsolescence, **a practice whereby products are designed to have a limited period of usefulness**, has been a cornerstone of manufacturing strategy for the past 80 years.

    Everything in bold is the additional info that also restates the same thing.

11. Answer is C.

The summer of 2012 was the warmest in 170 years, records show. But Jason Box, **an associate professor of geology at Ohio State**, believes that another factor added to the early thaw: the "dark snow" problem.

The bold is giving us more information about Jason Box, a man with a proper name meaning the additional info on him is not necessary.

12. Answer is D.

On the plane's ascent, passengers feel twice Earth's gravitational pull, but for brief periods at the peak of the trajectory, "weightlessness," **or microgravity similar to what is experienced in space**, is achieved.

The information in bold is a simple restating of what "weightlessness" is.

Okay, that's most of the stuff you need to know for commas. Just one more thing.

Here's a Rule: Use a comma to separate two adjectives when the adjectives are interchangeable.

Correct: He is a **strong, healthy** man. (Uses a comma)

> We could also say **healthy, strong** man.

Correct: We stayed at an **expensive summer** resort. (No comma)

> We could NOT say **summer expensive** resort.

In the first example, the adjectives are "interchangeable", meaning we could just switch them around and the sentence would still make sense. **So, we use a comma!**

In the second example, the adjectives cannot just be switched around. Then, the sentence would be nonsense. **So, we DON'T use a comma!**

Practice:

Punctuate the following sentences correctly.

1. The strong agile cat slept soundly.
2. The violently angry man shouted.
3. The violent angry man shouted.
4. I plan to attend the world-renowned elite Vohra Academy.
5. I go to a Batman fighting class.
6. The girl with the bright friendly smile wore a bright green scarf to celebrate St. Patrick's Day.
7. Having decided to eat only natural foods, he had to give up all of his favorite junk food snacks.
8. She listened to her favorite record with close careful attention.
9. Go to the first traffic light, turn left, and then look for a yellow brick building on the north side of the street.

10. It's the beginning of February, and as they do every year, thousands of people line H Street, the heart of Chinatown in Washington, DC. The crowd has gathered to celebrate Lunar New Year. The street is a sea of red, the traditional Chinese color of luck and happiness. Buildings are **draped with festive, red, banners,** and garlands. Lampposts are strung with crimson paper lanterns, which bob in the crisp winter breeze. The eager spectators await the highlight of the New Year parade: the lion dance.

    (A) NO CHANGE
    (B) draped, with festive red banners,
    (C) draped with festive red banners—
    (D) draped with festive red banners

Answers:

1. The strong, agile cat slept soundly.
2. The violently angry man shouted. **(No commas)**
3. The violent, angry man shouted.
4. I plan to attend the world-renowned, elite Vohra Academy.
5. I go to a Batman fighting class. **(No commas)**
6. The girl with the bright, friendly smile wore a bright green scarf to celebrate St. Patrick's Day. **(Only commas in the first set, not at "bright green"!)**
7. Having decided to eat only natural foods, he had to give up all of his favorite junk food snacks. **(No commas)**
8. She listened to her favorite record with close, careful attention.
9. Go to the first traffic light, turn left, and then look for a yellow brick building on the north side of the street. **(You wouldn't say "brick yellow building", so no commas!)**
10. Answer is D. We wouldn't say "red festive banners" and so we don't use commas.

Comma Such As

Here's the rule: Whenever you see "such as", take out the words "such as" along with the listed examples. If whatever is left makes sense, then you need commas! If whatever is left does NOT make sense, or changes the meaning of the sentence, then do NOT use commas.

Let's use examples to clarify.

Correct: You'll see many types of coniferous trees in this forest, such as pine and spruce.

Take out "such as pine and spruce".

[You'll see many types of coniferous trees in this forest] makes sense. It can be a complete sentence on its own. Therefore, we use a comma.

Wrong: Trees, such as oaks and elms, don't grow at this altitude.

Take out "such as oaks and elms".

[Trees don't grow at this altitude] is NOT what the original sentence meant. Some trees grow, just not these particular trees. We should NOT use commas.

Correct: Trees such as oaks and elms don't grow at this altitude.

Be sure that you're not changing the meaning of the sentence!

Practice:

1. Citrus fruits such as oranges and grapefruits are high in vitamin C.

2. We like to plan our vacations around three-day weekends, such as Labor Day.

3. Foods, such as pizza and ice cream, aren't very good for you.

4. This year we'd like to visit an exciting place such as Greece or Rome.

5. During periods of economic recession, public libraries and librarians are especially valuable, because they offer free resources that may be difficult to find elsewhere, such as help with online job searches as well as résumé and job material development.

6. Greek yogurt can be found in an increasing number of products, such as snack food and frozen desserts.

7. The spaces are usually stocked with standard office equipment such as photocopiers, printers, and fax machines.

Answers:

1. Citrus fruits, such as oranges and grapefruits, are high in vitamin C. **(needs commas)**

2. We like to plan our vacations around three-day weekends, such as Labor Day. **(Correct)**

3. Foods such as pizza and ice cream aren't very good for you. **(Correct, should not have commas)**

4. This year we'd like to visit an exciting place, such as Greece or Rome. **(needs commas)**

5. During periods of economic recession, public libraries and librarians are especially valuable, because they offer free resources that may be difficult to find elsewhere, such as help with online job searches as well as résumé and job material development. **(Correct)**

6. Greek yogurt can be found in an increasing number of products, such as snack food and frozen desserts. **(Correct)**

7. The spaces are usually stocked with standard office equipment, such as photocopiers, printers, and fax machines. **(needs commas)**

Semicolons

The rule for semicolons is easy. **You MUST have one complete, independent clause on each side of the semicolon.**

Wrong: Independent Clause; Dependent Clause
Wrong: Dependent Clause; Independent Clause
Right: Independent Clause; Independent Clause

Further Point! The two clauses MUST be **closely related**.

Correct: Call me tomorrow; you can give me an answer then.
Correct: We have paid our dues; we expect all the privileges listed in the contract.
Incorrect: I am tired; some trees are tall.

One extra, important note for these: The SAT Reading section will pull passages from history when the grammar and punctuation rules were different (especially for semicolons). Don't use older passages to learn grammar or punctuation. In fact, don't even use modern day passages, texts, or stories to learn grammar. I read plenty of books every month that have some bad grammar somewhere. Novels tend to take creative license with punctuation rules. TV shows and movies are just the worst. And remember, your friends, peers, and even family probably won't be good resources either. The sad fact is that America has failed in its instruction of grammar and has pretty much given up on it.

If you want to learn grammar, get a grammar rules book or find grammar rules online. There, you can be reasonably confident that the writer knows correct, modern grammar rules and will follow them.

Practice:

Explain why the following three examples are incorrect:

1. **Incorrect:** When we have paid our dues; we will expect all the privileges listed in the contract.

2. **Incorrect:** That boy is annoying; when he smashes into my fence.

3. **Incorrect:** Sarah is a teacher; oranges are tasty.

Answers:

1. "when we have paid our dues" is a dependent clause, not independent. You can only join two independent clauses.

2. "when he smashes into my fence" is a dependent clause.

3. The two clauses are not related.

Practice: Comma vs Semicolon

Insert the necessary punctuation in the following.

1. Many companies make sugar-free soft drinks which are flavored by synthetic chemicals the drinks usually contain only one or two calories per serving.
2. Mr. Leyland played the viola professionally for many years and now he conducts a community orchestra.
3. The crab grass was flourishing but the rest of the lawn unfortunately was dying.
4. The hill was covered with wildflowers it was a beautiful sight.
5. As I turned around I heard a loud thump the cat had upset the goldfish bowl.
6. The artist preferred to paint in oils he did not like watercolors.
7. The house was clean the table set and the porch light on everything was ready for the guests' arrival.
8. He looked carefully in the underbrush but he failed to notice the pair of green eyes staring at him.
9. The foundations of the house had been poured but nothing else had been done because of the carpenters' strike.

10. I liked the experience so much that I now go to the coworking space a few times a week. Over time, I've gotten to know several of my coworking ⭐ **colleagues;** ⭐ another website developer, a graphic designer, a freelance writer, and several mobile app coders. Even those of us who work in disparate fields are able to share advice and help each other brainstorm. In fact, it's the diversity of their talents and experiences that makes my coworking colleagues so valuable.

Explain why the bolded portion above is wrong. *(If you want, you can guess what the punctuation should be. You haven't learned all of the punctuation yet, though!)*

11. It took me by surprise, then, when my favorite exhibit at the museum was one of ⭐ **its tiniest;** ⭐ the Thorne Miniature Rooms.

Explain why the bolded portion above is wrong. *(If you want, you can guess what the punctuation should be. You haven't learned all of the punctuation yet, though!)*

12.

13. But they suggest that the presence of otters provides a good model of how carbon can be sequestered, **or removed; from** the atmosphere through the management of animal populations.

Explain why the bolded portion above is wrong. *(If you want, you can guess what the punctuation should be. You haven't learned all of the punctuation yet, though!)*

14. Because digital systems record **indiscriminately; they** cannot discern important parts of the proceedings from other noises in the courtroom.

Explain why the bolded portion above is wrong. *(If you want, you can guess what the punctuation should be. You haven't learned all of the punctuation yet, though!)*

Answers:

1. Many companies make sugar-free soft drinks which are flavored by synthetic chemicals; the drinks usually contain only one or two calories per serving. **(Semicolon)**

2. Mr. Leyland played the viola professionally for many years, and now he conducts a community orchestra. **(Comma)**

3. The crab grass was flourishing, but the rest of the lawn unfortunately was dying. **(Comma)**

4. The hill was covered with wildflowers; it was a beautiful sight. **(Semicolon)**

5. As I turned around, I heard a loud thump; the cat had upset the goldfish bowl. **(a comma and a semicolon)**

6. The artist preferred to paint in oils; he did not like watercolors. **(Semicolon)**

7. The house was clean, the table set, and the porch light on; everything was ready for the guests' arrival. **(Commas and a Semicolon)**

8. He looked carefully in the underbrush, but he failed to notice the pair of green eyes staring at him. **(Comma)**

9. The foundations of the house had been poured, but nothing else had been done because of the carpenters' strike. **(Comma)**

10. You can't use a semicolon to separate a clause and a list of things (aka, not a clause).

    Over time, I've gotten to know several of my coworking colleagues: another website developer, a graphic designer, a freelance writer, and several mobile app coders.

Technically, this would be a colon (as shown above). You'll learn about colons shortly.

11. You can't use a semicolon to separate a clause and a single noun.

    It took me by surprise, then, when my favorite exhibit at the museum was one of its tiniest: the Thorne Miniature Rooms.

    This one would also be a colon.

12. "from the atmosphere through the management of animal populations" isn't an independent clause.

    But they suggest that the presence of otters provides a good model of how carbon can be sequestered, or removed, from the atmosphere through the management of animal populations.

    This one is a comma. Actually, two commas surrounding the restating of "sequestered".

13. The word "because" makes that first clause dependent.

    Because digital systems record indiscriminately, they cannot discern important parts of the proceedings from other noises in the courtroom.

    This one would be a comma.

Recap: Semicolons separate two independent clauses; commas separate pretty much everything else. ALSO! Commas are NOT allowed to separate independent clauses.

(Ever heard of a comma splice or a run-on sentence? That's the error those refer to.)

Colons

Colons have one rule; **they introduce something**.

They can introduce a list.

I want to get the following from the store: blueberries, bananas, spinach.

But, more commonly on the SAT, they introduce a person or thing **that is described**.

I want to meet the enigmatic man stealing the spotlight in the space and technology worlds today: Elon Musk.

OR more simply

He got what he worked for: success.

In this usage, there is a description or introduction before or after the colon.

Wrong: The most important part of my day: the morning.
Neither side contains an independent clause, so it's not a sentence.

Also Wrong: One thing that really matters to me is: punctuation.
This is not how we use colons.

Practice:

Fill in the following with the appropriate punctuation.

1. There was one thing left to do arrive with excitement.

2. Jason Box, an associate professor of geology at Ohio State, believes that another factor added to the early thaw the "dark snow" problem.

3. The new style was loathsome to older designers they all knew the importance of the innovations made by younger stylists.

4. Over time, I've gotten to know several of my colleagues a website developer, a graphic designer, a freelance writer, and several mobile app coders.

5. Drawing on years of experience with this formation the coach felt he knew exactly what he wanted to do.

6. He worked at the factory for thirty years he never once got a promotion.

7. The spaces are usually stocked with standard office equipment, such as photocopiers, printers, and fax machines.

8. It took me by surprise, then, when my favorite exhibit at the museum was one of ✶ **it's tiniest;** ✶ the Thorne Miniature Rooms.

    (A) NO CHANGE
    (B) its tiniest;
    (C) its tiniest:
    (D) it's tiniest,

145

9. The plainer rooms are more sparsely **furnished: their** architectural features, furnishings, and decorations are just as true to the periods they represent.

Explain why the bolded portion above is wrong.

Answers:

1. There was one thing left to do: arrive with excitement.

2. Jason Box, an associate professor of geology at Ohio State, believes that another factor added to the early thaw: the "dark snow" problem.

3. The new style was loathsome to older designers; they all knew the importance of the innovations made by younger stylists. **(Semicolon! Not a colon!)**

4. Over time, I've gotten to know several of my colleagues: a website developer, a graphic designer, a freelance writer, and several mobile app coders.

5. Drawing on years of experience with this formation, the coach felt he knew exactly what he wanted to do. **(Comma!)**

6. He worked at the factory for thirty years; he never once got a promotion. **(Semicolon)**

7. The spaces are usually stocked with standard office equipment, such as photocopiers, printers, and fax machines. **(Correct as is. This is how we use [comma such as])**

8. Answer is C.

9. This should be a semicolon.

Now, of course the SAT can't just use the normal colon. It has to use the weird and confusing colons!

Colons **can** also be used in the same place that you might use a semicolon or a period, because of course they can. English is weird and sometimes annoying in it's rules and caveats.

Here's an example:

Just weeks after the scientists added the nitrates and phosphates, the water in Lake 227 turned bright **green. It was thick with:** the same type of algal blooms that had plagued Lake Erie.

- **(A)** NO CHANGE
- **(B)** green: it was thick with
- **(C)** green. It was thick with—
- **(D)** green, it was thick with

For this a question like this, you might immediately look for a semicolon…and there isn't one. You could, then, go into pure Disprove; Don't Prove mode. This is what I encourage my students to do.

But also know that you can use a colon here, even though there are two Independent Clauses, one on either side of the punctuation.

Disproving:

The way it's written, you wouldn't even put a comma there, much less a period or semicolon. And therefore not a colon either.

It obviously can't be a dash, there would need to be a pair of those.

If you only use a comma, it would be a comma splice! (You can't join Independent Clauses with only a comma.)

So, that leaves us with B. It's a weird non-rule thing, so just stick with Disproving and you'll get it.

Parentheses and Dashes

Really what you need to know for these is that they always come in pairs.

How will the SAT try to trick you? They will create questions where the pair of parentheses or dashes will be far away from each other in the sentence, and the question will only be asking about one of them. So, if you don't notice that there was a dash before…you'll get it wrong.

Parentheses look like this: (stuff)

Dashes look like this: —stuff—

You can generally use them interchangeably.

The committee's first attempt to reduce the angle of the tower's tilt—placing 600 tons of iron ingots (molded pieces of metal) on the tower's north side to create a counterweight—was derided because the bulky weights ruined the tower's appearance.

The committee's first attempt to reduce the angle of the tower's tilt (placing 600 tons of iron ingots (molded pieces of metal) on the tower's north side to create a counterweight) was derided because the bulky weights ruined the tower's appearance.

Either of those is technically fine, but if you use parentheses, then you have two sets of parentheses. That creates some mild confusion, so it's better to use dashes.

Practice:

Fix these up, if they need fixing!

1. The attempt at a less visible solution, sinking anchors into the ground below the tower—almost caused the tower to fall.

2. Because a traditionalist response to the crisis—bolstering medical-college enrollments and expanding physician training programs; is too slow and costly to address the near-term problem, alternatives are being explored.

3. Moreover, the training period for PAs is markedly shorter than that for physicians—two to three years versus the seven to eleven required for physicians.

Answers:

1. The attempt at a less visible solution—sinking anchors into the ground below the tower—almost caused the tower to fall.

2. Because a traditionalist response to the crisis—bolstering medical-college enrollments and expanding physician training programs—is too slow and costly to address the near-term problem, alternatives are being explored.

3. Moreover, the training period for PAs is markedly shorter than that for physicians—two to three years versus the seven to eleven required for physicians. **(Correct as is)**

I like this one because it forces you all to think. Dashes can be used just like parentheses. With parentheses, you might write something like:

Moreover, the training period for PAs is markedly shorter than that for physicians (two to three years versus the seven to eleven required for physicians).

But, with dashes, you wouldn't put a dash out there at the end, just before a period. You just need the one to start the offset information!

Little More Practice:

Answer the following.

1. Indeed, when we think about animals depicted in well-known works of art, the image of dogs playing poker—popularized in a series of paintings by American artist C. M. **Coolidge,** may be the first and only one that comes to mind.

    (A) NO CHANGE
    (B) Coolidge—
    (C) Coolidge;
    (D) Coolidge

2. Boss Tweed's Tammany Hall group, which controlled New York **City in the 1860s—** stole more than $30 million, the equivalent of more than $365 million today.

    (A) NO CHANGE
    (B) City in the 1860s,
    (C) City, in the 1860s,
    (D) City in the 1860s

3. In addition to super villains, the new, soon-to-be-iconic characters of the **age:** Spider-Man, the Fantastic Four, and the Hulk among them—had to cope with mundane, real-life problems, including paying the rent, dealing with family squabbles, and facing anger, loneliness, and ostracism.

    (A) NO CHANGE
    (B) age;
    (C) age,
    (D) age—

4. It is not difficult to understand why a cash-strapped, understaffed publication might feel pressure to cut teams of investigative **reporter's—** their work is expensive and time-consuming.

   (A) NO CHANGE
   (B) reporters:
   (C) reporters,
   (D) reporter's;

Answers:

1. **B**
There's already one dash, so you need another.

2. **B**
This one does not have another dash, so we need to take the current one out and use a comma!

3. **D**
Needs a pair of dashes.

4. **B**
This question is a bit ugly, which is why I included it. For the record, I don't like this question. I think it's important that you learn that the SAT makers are human and fallible. Sometimes they make bad questions.

This situation is not a common use for a colon. Most people wouldn't use a colon this way; they'd use a semicolon. BUT, the option that has the semicolon also has an incorrect usage of possessive vs plural. So, you just have to think through the best worst option.

Reading Crossover

This section comes from my Three-Week SAT Crash Course for Reading. The Grammar section of the SAT is just a bunch of passages now, so your ability to simplify what you read into digestible bits is very important. I'm including my discussion of the Simple Ridiculous Summary here and we'll explore how it applies in the Grammar section later on.

I'm also including my discussion of Disprove; Don't Prove. I'm keeping these discussions identical in both books so that you know you only have to read it once. You will need these skills for BOTH Reading and Grammar. If you're simultaneously studying for Reading, then this will serve a dual purpose!

You should read over these sections and do the exercises contained within.

The Simple Ridiculous Summary

You need to make the SAT reading passages more SIMPLE, not more complex!

Good grief, if I told you some of the crazy, convoluted, mental-gymnastics-style answers I've gotten to the simplest of questions...well, hopefully we would share a good laugh.

You know if you're a student who does this. When asked a question in English class, 40% of your answer is just an elaborate and circuitous rephrasing of the question, followed by an elaborate and circuitous re-ordering of so many words from the passage that it sort of sounds like you know what you're saying. In reality, you're just making a Frankenstein monster out of the passage, hoping that the more complex and unreadable your answer looks (boy do you LOVE the thesaurus!) the better your grade will be.

Now, here's the kicker.

The more you made your answers complex and unreadable and full of 15 letter synonyms for simple words...the better your grades got!!

I've always said that high school in America these days doesn't teach you much, and most of it you forget with just a little break, but the one skill high schools across the nation never fail to teach is how to bullshit.

My point is this: It's not your fault. Literally NONE of your current SAT situation is your fault. Your whole life, people told you, "If you do this, you'll be smart." "If you do this, you'll get into a good college." "If you do this, you'll get a good job, make good money, and have a good life."

I won't get into all the flaws in those statements. You're probably already waking up to the harsh reality of college admissions.

The point is, those people lied to you. Everything they made you do did NOT prepare you for what, in reality, is a pretty basic test of Algebra, English grammar, and critical reading.

It's not your fault that you're starting where you are. But, after reading this book, your next score will be your fault (**and your own proud achievement**).

How do we combat what your school has taught you for 13 years (or so)?

It's actually pretty simple, but it will probably be physically painful at first. You have to create the Simple, Ridiculous Summary (the SRS).

But Chelsey, I've done summaries before. That doesn't sound too bad!

Well, there's a twist. The most important rule of the SRS is that you specifically MUST make your English teacher cry. If your English teacher read this summary, not only would she give you an F-, she would also immediately burst into tears!

Why?

Because, your school taught you how to read in such a convoluted way that you can't even answer a simple question simply! So, whatever your school thinks is a "simple" summary...it ain't.

And how do we create this SRS?

Easy, use English bad.

If there's a passage about scientists who are studying the activity of a particular volcano, and they don't know why this one volcano erupted so much earlier than anticipated, and they want to use that information to create a model for other, less predictable volcanoes...then you write, "Earth made a surprise 'splosion and scientists be like, what it do?!"

Use crazy words like ain't, gon' (meaning going to), fam, lit...

Use silly phrases like 'what it do' and 'up in here' and 'be like'. One of my favorites is "ain't nobody got time for that."

The point is to make your summary chill. The way you would describe a book to your bros or your gals.

Ain't nobody up in here like, "My dearest compatriot. Thineself shouldst peruse Twilight, a new text which encompasses the woes of a teenaged female attempting to procure for herself an interest of endearment who is neither a homo sapiens nor a matte-skinned fellow."

You guys have got to loosen up... I hope at this point you're having a good laugh at yourself, because I definitely am!

So, here are the specific requirements:

How to write the SRS (Simple, Ridiculous Summary)

1. You must use the phrase "**be like**". (It basically means "says" or "thinks".)
2. You must use **no more than two sentences**.
3. Your summary must be **comprehensible to a 5-year-old**.
4. Your summary **must NOT include any of the words from the passage**.

So, make it ridiculous. Use crazy phrases. Keep it very short (as short as possible, only 1 sentence is perfectly acceptable). Really boil the ideas down. Everything can be explained, on some level, to a 5-year-old. You can make it that simple, and you should. And whatever you do, don't just pull 50 words from the passage, stick them in a hat, jumble them up, and spit them back out as some kind of pseudo-intelligence. We will have none of that!

How to Use Your SRS:

After you practice with this skill a bit (practice exercises will come at the end of this chapter), you'll be wondering, "but, how does this help me?"

First, there is very often a question on at least 3 of the 5 SAT passages that will directly ask you for a summary. It might ask for a summary of just the first paragraph. It might ask something like, "How does the passage progress?" You'll often see questions asking about the main idea. All of these things will relate back to your simple summary.

But then, there will be questions you wouldn't expect that will lean heavily into just a basic, surface level understanding of the passage. This is especially true in the fiction passages, where emotions and human motivations are key. Things like deception, too, would stand out in your SRS. And, if your SRS is good, then you'll find one answer choice clearly describing whatever deception or intention or desire you pinpointed. It's hard to spot at first, but you can get it with practice.

You'll find a specific, partnered exercise on this later in the chapter. Just keep this mantra in mind: When in doubt, go back to your Simple, Ridiculous Summary.

How to Practice:

First, you WILL need practice on this. Everything above sounds so simple (if a bit silly); I know. But, every student I have worked with **always** immediately reverts back to his/her old ways. It takes about 10 seconds for students to give me summaries that are 150-word-long run-on sentences, or just 8 sentences long, or contain entire 20-word QUOTES from the passage! And it takes everyone a while to get used to the physical uncomfortableness of using bad English when you think you're supposed to be studying English.

I get it; this is weird. It's weird, and it works. I've helped students improve their reading scores by 120+ points in 6 hours of tutoring. If you're looking for a "magic spell" that will get you an amazing score very, very fast...this is the closest thing you'll find.

But, you have to commit to it. You have to actually follow the requirements for the SRS. You have to actually make a SRS for every passage. You need to practice.

If you want to practice with SAT passages, you really need some external person to rigorously tell you if your SRS is too complex, too short-sighted, too long, etc. If you want to work with me, you can visit VohraMethod.com. Otherwise, find the most renegade person you know and show them the requirements, then show them your summary attempts.

You can't use your teachers; they'll just tell you that your English is bad, and they'll start crying (that's the point!). You can't use your parents (sorry mom and dad) because they will also be very off-put by the poor English and silly phrases. If, by chance, your mom or dad is super renegade, then use them.

You need someone who reads a lot, and who isn't afraid to break the rules. The "rules" of your life have been that if you put out terrible summaries that are basically longer than the passage and equally as dense, then you win. On the SAT, you do that...you lose.

Exercise: Rely on the SRS

1. Get a partner. Pick someone who is smart, has read this book, and is trying to get a perfect SAT score (no slackers allowed!).
2. Get a Barron's SAT book with practice tests. DO NOT use the official College Board tests for this! Those are limited, and you need them for your official practice.
3. Pick out two fiction passages. These will come from two separate tests. You take one; your partner takes one.
4. Both of you read your passage and make your best SRS.
5. Give your partner the questions from your passage (which he/she has not read), and also pass over your SRS. Your partner will now attempt to answer as many questions as possible using ONLY the SRS (no reading the passage!). You do the same with your partner's passage.
6. Don't expect to get all of the questions right, obviously. But, you will get SOME of them right. This is very powerful, and it will help you build up the right intuition to dominate the SAT.
7. Repeat this exercise for each passage type. You should both do science passages at the same time, dual passages at the same time, etc.

Basically, practice as much as you possibly can until your test date. The SAT will matter more than almost anything else you put in your college application. If you're trying to get recruited for a sport, your SAT score will matter about 100 times more than all school grades, extracurriculars, and college essays combined because they need to keep their SAT averages up for the team as a whole.

Just keep practicing and don't stop until your test day. If you can't find a partner, you can come hang out with me. You can also practice your SRS on books that you read for fun, on news articles and journals, on anything.

Disprove; Don't Prove

Due to your upbringing in a school environment, you're probably used to writing "essays". This is basically where you pretend to read a miserable book that you hate, then you pick out quotes from that book (basically at random) and you use those quotes to "prove" some kind of terrible thesis. This is all no offense to you, obviously. The offense is all to your school. But, sadly, this process has taught you three things:

1. How to write something that is almost certainly NOT a thesis.
2. How to use pretty much ANY evidence to prove ANY claim.
3. How to bullshit.

Now, the value of #3 is arguable, but the big problem we have for the SAT is #2. You are so used to using any nonsensical evidence to prove any ridiculous claim that you are going to get things wrong on the test IF you use the same methods.

Here's how this usually plays out:

Mental Gymnastics:

Well, in the passage, Bob is wearing a yellow tie. Yellow is the color of springtime and hope. The springtime is when the world comes alive again. New trees, baby animals, pretty flowers. But it's winter in this story right now. So, either Bob is having a baby (new birth/springtime), or Bob is confused and has conflicting emotions.

Let's all stop and take a moment to laugh at this nonsense.

HAAHHAHhahahaahahaha

Okay great. But here's the deal. You have DEFinitely done this in your own brain before. **Every single one of my students** has done it live in front of me! You've probably done it so many times that it doesn't even seem weird anymore.

Schools have gone so heavy on symbolism and "deeper meaning" that they've contorted "reading" into a task where you basically just make stuff up that the author maybe/probably/definitely never intended. Schools have turned reading into an interpretation act, instead of an opportunity to access the sharp mind of another individual.

And, as always, you are the one who suffers. First, because no one enjoys an interpretation act where one person pretends he/she knows THE answer. And second, because now you're failing the SAT.

On the SAT, things are a lot more straightforward. They sort of have to be, and you should understand why.

If it ever came out that the College Board (the company making the test) were creating subjective questions, questions that could arguably be either A or B, or maybe even C, depending on how you "interpret" the passage...well, you can be sure that a lot of parents would draw up a class action lawsuit quick, fast, and in a big hurry.

They simply cannot create ambiguous questions. There's always a clear reason why the answer is B, not A.

So, why do you have to disprove, not prove?

Because you're very used to proving nonsense using nonsense. But, you're not very used to DISproving at all. Most students don't do a lot of Proof by Contradiction, and your school is less interested in your disproving false claims about a passage than in proving whatever new fluffy idea **might** be true about whatever boring book.

This is great! It means you have a tool you can use. And, it turns out, almost every one of my students in many years of tutoring has been terrible at proving, but pretty great at disproving!

Key Skill: Disprove Using ONE Word

This is just an extension of Disprove Don't Prove, and it's intended to help focus your efforts. If even one, tiny fraction of an answer choice is wrong, then that entire answer choice is super wrong, so don't pick it.

Here's an example answer choice:

(A) says "the narrator's attitude shifts from fear about the expedition to excitement about it".

So, we ask ourselves, is the narrator showing "fear"? If not, then A is wrong.

If the narrator is showing fear, then is that fear "about the expedition" or about something else? If it's about something else, then A is wrong.

If the fear is about the expedition, then we see if he's showing "excitement".

If he is showing excitement, then we see if the excitement is about "the expedition".

And, if all those things are true, then we need to ask if the narrator shifts "from" the fear "to" the excitement. In other words, is the narrator afraid at the beginning of the passage, and excited at the end? If the order is reversed, then A is wrong.

I know that seems like a lot of steps, but you'll pick it up quickly. For my students, just knowing that there are clear steps and progressive questions you can ask yourself seems to assuage a lot of the anxiety around the test questions and answers.

Key Skill: Ask Yourself, "What would _____ look like?"

Sometimes you're stuck between two answers. Actually, that probably happens a lot! When you get to that place, this skill can be really helpful.

Also, for some mystical reason, almost every single student I've worked with is just magically good at this skill with little to no practice. It's a simple idea, so be sure to keep it simple!

You just ask yourself, "What would it look like if A were true?"

Here's an example answer choice:

The sentence in lines 10-13 mainly serves to...

(B) demonstrate that the narrator thinks in a methodical and scientific manner.

Ask yourself, "If the passage were really trying to show that Dudeface McGee 'thinks in a methodical and scientific manner', what would that look like?"

Well, you'd probably see him approaching a problem and thinking it through. He would probably use a lot of If Then statements, or maybe create a hypothesis and then a test for that hypothesis.

You guys all KNOW what science looks like, at least at a basic level. Hypothesis, test, controls, variables, results, conclusion.

You also KNOW what a method looks like.

Remember, **this book is about unlocking your inherent superpowers.** So, work with what you know.

Side note: the more you know, the better your whole life will generally be. Knowledge is gained by books.

Read more books! But, specifically not any of the books your school recommends. Some of them might not be terrible, but they are probably all very boring. If you want some book recommendations, send me an email. I can give you a ton of ideas completely free.

We're going to practice Disprove Don't Prove very soon. Generally, you should practice it in every practice test and passage you read.

Test 1 Grammar Section – Crossover Questions

Before you start getting into tests, keep this in mind: The grammar section is ALSO a test of reading. As you read, you should retain the information that the passage is teaching you. Sure, there aren't any "main idea" questions, but there are questions about ordering sentences, using correct transition words, providing the right details and examples **to support the main argument,** etc. So, don't disengage from the information while trying to figure out the grammatical rules.

In fact! On the College Board's first SAT practice test, there are a full 15 out of 44 questions that talk about sentence ordering, adding a sentence, transition words, logically connecting two sentences or paragraphs, etc. Those are all reading questions. That's over one third of the questions on the grammar section!

So, don't be fooled. Next, we'll do the critical reading types of questions, vocabulary questions, and chart analysis questions (bit of a crossover with math).

Most of the other types of questions from Test 1 were spread out through the sections you've already read (Selected Skills, Punctuation, etc.). You'll continue to practice those skills in future tests!

Note: For this test, you'll see the questions in big black circle numbers. Then, the underlined portion will be the portion in question. I'll also put stars around the part that we're immediately focusing on.

I strongly recommend going to College Board's site and downloading their official copy of Practice Test 1. It helps to have the test and the questions and discussion side by side. You can access that test here: https://collegereadiness.collegeboard.org/sat/practice/full-length-practice-tests

Reading Comprehension Questions

Whey to Go

Greek yogurt—a strained form of cultured yogurt—has grown enormously in popularity in the United States since it was first introduced in the country in the late 1980s.

From 2011 to 2012 alone, sales of Greek yogurt in the US increased by 50 percent. The resulting increase in Greek yogurt production has forced those involved in the business to address the detrimental effects that the yogurt-making process may be having on the environment. Fortunately, farmers and others in the Greek yogurt business have found many methods of controlling and eliminating most environmental threats. Given these solutions as well as the many health benefits of the food, the advantages of Greek yogurt ❶ outdo the potential drawbacks of its production.

[1] The main environmental problem caused by the production of Greek yogurt is the creation of acid whey as a by-product. [2] Because it requires up to four times more milk to make than conventional yogurt does, Greek yogurt produces larger amounts of acid whey, which is difficult to dispose of. [3] To address the problem of disposal, farmers have found a number of uses for acid whey. [4] They can add it to livestock feed as a protein ❷ supplement, and people can make their own Greek-style yogurt at home by straining regular yogurt. [5] If it is improperly introduced into the environment, acid-whey runoff ❸ can pollute waterways, depleting the oxygen content of streams and rivers as it decomposes. [6] Yogurt manufacturers, food ❹ scientists; and government officials are also working together to develop additional solutions for reusing whey. ❺

2 Which choice provides the most relevant detail?

   (A) NO CHANGE
   (B) supplement and convert it into gas to use as fuel in electricity production.
   (C) supplement, while sweet whey is more desirable as a food additive for humans.
   (D) supplement, which provides an important element of their diet.

Go ahead and take a guess, then we'll discuss.

Now I'll ask you a very simple question that I can virtually **guarantee** you did not ask yourself:

Based on the surrounding sentences, what sorts of details is sentence 4 supposed to contain?

Go ahead and answer now, on paper.

It's supposed to contain "disposal uses for acid whey".

Disposal use number 1: Add it to livestock feed as a protein supplement.

What should disposal use number 2 be? Something that we can do with acid whey (a byproduct of creating Greek yogurt).

Options for disposal use number 2:

- **(A)** people can make their own Greek-style yogurt at home by straining regular yogurt
- **(B)** convert it into gas to use as fuel in electricity production.
- **(C)** sweet whey is more desirable as a food additive for humans.
- **(D)** provides an important element of [the livestock's] diet.

Answer is B.

A isn't about acid whey at all. C is about sweet whey, which is totally different. D isn't a second example of disposal methods, it's just an elaboration on the first disposal method. The prior sentence said:

To address the problem of disposal, farmers have found **a number of uses** for acid whey.

"Uses" is plural. So, we need to list at LEAST two uses...

Now, around this point is when most of my students say, "OHHHHH, of course! Ya, of course that totally makes sense, yepp, for sure. I definitely totally understand this and don't even know why I got it wrong, lolz."

But here's the problem: They just keep on getting these types of "super obvious" questions wrong.

Why?

Because they haven't fully trained their brains to ask questions. And, you probably haven't either. That's why you're here.

You probably think that you're taking these tests, reading all the questions, and answering the questions on the page. But, most of the time…you aren't. Most of the time, when students get questions wrong, they don't even know why they picked whichever answer they picked, nor do they seem to understand what the question was asking, what the answer choice says, or what the passage was even vaguely about.

Our brains tend to immediately disengage from things we find boring, tedious, or unimportant for basic survival. The SAT hits just about every box. Ever find yourself having to reread an SAT passage or sentence for the third time, panicking that you're going to run out of time but just unable to focus on the sentence at hand? This is why. And the tools to combat this are very simple.

Ask yourself questions. Talk to yourself.

If you maintain a conversation with yourself about the SAT while you're taking it, you'll stay more engaged and more focused. If you don't, your mind will wander.

So, when the question says, "Which choice provides the most relevant detail?", you should ask yourself, "What details should this sentence contain?". Simple enough question, and it brings you back into the passage and the real question at hand. We'll practice throughout this book.

[1] The main environmental problem caused by the production of Greek yogurt is the creation of acid whey as a by-product. [2] Because it requires up to four times more milk to make than conventional yogurt does, Greek yogurt produces larger amounts of acid whey, which is difficult to dispose of. [3] To address the problem of disposal, farmers have found a number of uses for acid whey. [4] They can add it to livestock feed as a protein ❷ <u>supplement, and people can make their own Greek-style yogurt at home by straining regular yogurt.</u> [5] If it is improperly introduced into the environment, acid-whey runoff ❸ <u>can pollute waterways,</u> depleting the oxygen content of streams and rivers as it decomposes. [6] Yogurt manufacturers, food ❹ <u>scientists; and</u> government officials are also working together to develop additional solutions for reusing whey. ❺

❺ To make this paragraph most logical, sentence 5 should be placed

- **(A)** Where it is now.
- **(B)** after sentence 1.
- **(C)** after sentence 2.
- **(D)** after sentence 3.

Try to think of a simple question you can ask yourself to get your brain engaged with this information in the right way. Then, select your answer and read on!

The question you should ask yourself for all sentence ordering questions is this: **What is the paragraph shifting FROM and TO?**

Most of the time, paragraphs will shift from one idea to another idea. Not unrelated ideas! It'll shift from a Cause to an Effect, or from a Problem to a Solution, or from a General idea to Specific examples. Something like that.

If you know what the passage is shifting From and To, then you can figure out if the sentence in question should be part of the From, part of the To, or part of the transition in between.

Figure out what this Whey paragraph is shifting From and To.

So, rereading the first sentence, we see the word "problem" right away. This is probably a Problem/Solution paragraph. Now we ask ourselves, what is each sentence doing? In other words, is it part of the Problem, the Solution, or the Transition?

Go ahead and write down your answers for each sentence.

Sentence 1: Problem
Sentence 2: Problem
Sentence 3: Transition from problem to solution
Sentence 4: Solution
Sentence 5: Problem
Sentence 6: Summary sentence about solutions

Already, we can see that sentence 5 cannot go where it is right now. We don't transition from discussing the Problem to discussing the Solution…and then jump back to the problem again really quickly…and then finish discussing solutions.

It needs to come before sentence 3 in order to be part of the discussion of the Problem, so that also rules out D.

Now, how do we decide between B and C? We dive deeper. Ask yourself, what **details** do those few sentences contain that can help me put them in order?

~Look at sentences 1, 2, 3, and 5. Find specific details.

Sentence 1: Tells us that acid whey is bad.
Sentence 2: Tells us that Greek yogurt production creates a lot of acid whey.
Sentence 3: Transitions into methods of disposal.
Sentence 5: Tells us that if acid whey isn't disposed of properly, then it is very bad.

Hopefully you can see that sentence 5 should go after sentence 2. It helps to get us into a discussion of disposal of this big whey problem.

Now, you're not going to take the time to write all that out on the real test. You just won't have that kind of time. BUT! You have to still engage on this level. You can write little P's and S's next to each sentence for Problem and Solution. You can write C's and E's for Cause and Effect, etc. And then you can (and must) still ask yourself, "What is each sentence doing? And what details are there worth noting?"

You can underline key nouns that indicate the details of each sentence. You can circle things and draw arrows, whatever. Personally, I think that "annotating" a text is just student-code for "I'm going to underline every single thing in the passage just in case it's important." In which case...I can help you out simply by typing Ctrl+A and Ctrl+U.

Underlining the whole passage is dumb and pointless; don't do that. But, underlining small details that can help you arrange the sentences can be very useful. **So, start practicing now!** You have to practice doing this in order to use it on test day. If you don't practice it A LOT (until it's muscle memory and automatic), then you won't actually do it on test day. You'll tell yourself to do it just before the test starts, and then everything will pop right out of your brain the second the proctor says "go".

High-stakes tests require habits training just as much as academic training. My goal in this book is to show you that there's not as much that you really have to **learn**. Much more so, you need to practice the habits that will help you tap into what you already know (and the few things you'll learn) on test day.

[1] Box's research is important because the fires of 2012 may not be a one-time phenomenon. [2] According to scientists, rising Arctic temperatures are making northern latitudes greener and thus more fire prone. [3] The pattern Box observed in 2012 may repeat ㉑ itself again, with harmful effects on the Arctic ecosystem. [4] Box is currently organizing an expedition to gather this crucial information. [5] The next step for Box and his team is to travel to Greenland to perform direct sampling of the ice in order to determine just how much the soot is contributing to the melting of the ice sheet. [6] Members of the public will be able to track his team's progress—and even help fund the expedition—through a website Box has created. ㉒

㉒ To make this paragraph most logical, sentence 4 should be placed

- **(A)** where it is now.
- **(B)** after sentence 1.
- **(C)** after sentence 2.
- **(D)** after sentence 5.

You know the drill. Ask yourself what this paragraph transitions From and To. Write it down!

This paragraph starts with a problem and transitions into a discussion of research that needs to be done. The research isn't exactly a solution, but it would be a step in the direction of a solution. So, for ease, we can call it Problem/Solution.

Now figure out what each sentence is about, the Problem or the Solution.

Sentence 1: Basic intro sentence, doesn't get into the problem yet.
Sentence 2: Problem
Sentence 3: Problem
Sentence 4: Research (Solution)
Sentence 5: Research (Solution)
Sentence 6: Totally separate closing sentence.

So, it's not immediately clear that sentence 4 should be moved around. We move from Problem to Solution, and that sounds good. We want sentence 4 to stay in the Research/Solution area, so either it should stay where it is, or it should switch places with sentence 5. That at least narrows it down to A and D.

Now what do we ask ourselves?

What details can help us determine order here?

The best detail here is a small one, but a common one! So, I'll point it out now, and you should stay on the lookout for it in the future.

It's the word "this".

Also, the words "that", "those", "them", "his/hers", etc. Pronouns!

When you have a pronoun, that pronoun has to refer to some noun. The noun can be in the same sentence OR in a sentence just prior. But, **the noun that the pronoun refers to will never be like 10 sentences away just chillin'.**

So, if you have a pronoun like "this" in sentence 4, then you need to make sure that the Antecedent of that pronoun is clear and in the preceding sentence, otherwise the order is wrong.

Sentence 3 tells us that Box did some research in 2012 and observed some stuff. Sentence 4 says that Box is organizing an expedition to gather **this crucial information**. What is "this crucial information"? Is it the observations he already observed in 2012? No, obviously not. So, sentence 4 must be in the wrong place.

Let's try it this way:

[5] The next step for Box and his team is to travel to Greenland to perform direct sampling of the ice **in order to determine just how much the soot is contributing** to the melting of the ice sheet. [4] Box is currently organizing an expedition to gather **this crucial information**.

Now it's very clear what "this crucial information" is.

Pro Tip: Always look for pronouns in the sentence ordering questions. They can make your life so easy!

[1] Thus, even though I already had all the equipment I needed in my home office, I decided to try using a coworking space in my city. [2] Because I was specifically interested in coworking's reported benefits related to creativity, I chose a facility that offered a bright, open work area where I wouldn't be isolated. [3] Throughout the morning, more people appeared. [4] Periods of quiet, during which everyone worked independently, were broken up occasionally with lively conversation.

31 The writer wants to add the following sentence to the paragraph.

After filling out a simple registration form and taking a quick tour of the facility, I took a seat at a table and got right to work on my laptop.

The best placement for the sentence is immediately

 (A) before sentence 1.
 (B) after sentence 1.
 (C) after sentence 2.
 (D) after sentence 3.

Figure out the flow of this paragraph first! Then pick an answer and read on.

So, this paragraph isn't moving from one thing to one other thing. This is just a sequence of events type thing. As in: I did this, then this, then this, and finally that.

Simplify the action that happens in each of these sentences.

[1] Thus, even though I already had all the equipment I needed in my home office, I decided to try using a coworking space in my city.

[2] Because I was specifically interested in coworking's reported benefits related to creativity, I chose a facility that offered a bright, open work area where I wouldn't be isolated.

[3] Throughout the morning, more people appeared.

[4] Periods of quiet, during which everyone worked independently, were broken up occasionally with lively conversation.

After filling out a simple registration form and taking a quick tour of the facility, I took a seat at a table and got right to work on my laptop.

[1] Decided to use coworking space.

[2] Chose a particular coworking space.

[3] Other people came to the coworking space.

[4] Work and conversation happened.

Arrived at the coworking place and got set up.

Think logically. When, in this sequence of events, is this guy going to arrive at the coworking space? Probably after he decides which place to go to and before he starts watching other people arrive there.

But, when you're looking at these more complex, long-winded sentences in the original passage, that can be harder to see. So, actually do something like this exercise we just did. Instead of writing out the action from each sentence, you could simply underline the MAIN verb and perhaps its subject. That will get you to roughly the same place.

The key here is to simplify everything. Don't make things more complicated to think about. Don't consider the details unless you're stuck between two answers. Don't consider adjectives until you need them for a tie-breaker. Just focus on the actions or the big topics at first.

And keep things simple in your own head! **DO NOT talk to yourself using the language of the passage.** That's not your language; that's not your lingo. Use silly phrases and slang terms. Use the words "…and stuff" a lot. Make it sound like caveman-speak. Make it sound like surfer-dude-bro-speak. Anything that makes it a little bit more silly and a LOT bit more simple…do that!

First Paragraph of the Passage: Greek yogurt—a strained form of cultured yogurt—has grown enormously in popularity in the United States since it was first introduced in the country in the late 1980s.

…(paragraph removed for brevity)

[1] The main environmental problem caused by the production of Greek yogurt is the creation of acid whey as a by-product. [2] Because it requires up to four times more milk to make than conventional yogurt does, Greek yogurt produces larger amounts of acid whey, which is difficult to dispose of. [3] To address the problem of disposal, farmers have found a number of uses for acid whey. [4] They can add it to livestock feed as a protein ❷ supplement, and people can make their own Greek-style yogurt at home by straining regular yogurt. [5] If it is improperly introduced into the environment, acid-whey runoff ❸ can pollute waterways, depleting the oxygen content of streams and rivers as it decomposes. [6] Yogurt manufacturers, food ❹ scientists; and government officials are also working together to develop additional solutions for reusing whey. ❺

✶ ❻ **Though these conservation methods can be costly and time-consuming, they are well worth the effort.** ✶ Nutritionists consider Greek yogurt to be a healthy food: it is an excellent source of calcium and protein, serves ❼ to be a digestive aid, and ❽ it contains few calories in its unsweetened low- and non-fat forms. Greek yogurt is slightly lower in sugar and carbohydrates than conventional yogurt is. ❾ Also, because it is more concentrated, Greek yogurt contains slightly more protein per serving, thereby helping people stay ❿ satiated for longer periods of time. These health benefits have prompted Greek yogurt's recent surge in popularity. In fact, Greek yogurt can be found in an increasing number of products such as snack food and frozen desserts. Because consumers reap the nutritional benefits of Greek yogurt and support those who make and sell ⓫ it, therefore farmers and businesses should continue finding safe and effective methods of producing the food.

6 The writer is considering deleting the bolded sentence. Should the writer do this?

(A) Yes, because it does not provide a transition from the previous paragraph.
(B) Yes, because it fails to support the main argument of the passage as introduced in the first paragraph.
(C) No, because it continues the explanation of how acid whey can be disposed of safely.
(D) No, because it sets up the argument in the paragraph for the benefits of Greek yogurt.

Similar idea to the sentence ordering questions. You need to ask yourself, "What are these two paragraphs shifting FROM and TO?" Let's first get an idea of what each paragraph is about. You get ONE simple sentence description per paragraph! And then also simplify the point of the sentence in question here.

Write down your answers to that now.

The first paragraph was about the problem of acid whey as a by-product and how they might be able to fix that problem.

This second paragraph, excluding the sentence in question, is about the health benefits of Greek yogurt (and therefore why the acid whey disposal efforts are still worth it).

The sentence in question says that even though the disposal effort might be a negative, it's worth it.

The paragraphs are shifting from "acid whey is bad" to "Greek yogurt is good". The sentence in question pretty much does the same!

Now, here's the big rule for this type of question: **Don't look at the "Yes" or "No" part of the answer choices.**

Most students, when they get these questions wrong, will pick one of the YES answers when it should be NO (or vice versa). Similarly, students will constantly pick a KEEP answer when it should be DELETE (and vice versa).

Because of this, I have made it a strong recommendation that all students completely ignore the starting word of each answer choice. Physically scribble out the words Yes and No if you want to. Just make sure you're not looking at them when you answer these questions.

Focus on the reasoning. Disproving will always be a more powerful tactic, based on how you've been taught so far in life. So, look through everything after the word "because" and find single words that you can disprove, or ask yourself what such things would look like.

>   **(A)** because it does not provide a transition from the previous paragraph.

This is false. The sentence does transition between the two paragraphs. We already looked at the topics of the two paragraphs and the content of this sentence.

Of course, if you didn't look at the overall content of each passage, and the content of the sentence in question, then you wouldn't necessarily see this. So, be sure to actively think about it.

(This skills becomes passive after about 100 hours of practice. If you only have three weeks, you'll have to maintain this skill actively the whole time.)

> **(B)** because it fails to support the main argument of the passage as introduced in the first paragraph.

This is why I included the first paragraph for this question. On a real test, you should quickly flip back to the passage and skim the first paragraph, obv.

The first paragraph says that Greek yogurt is getting more popular. The sentence in question is saying that the disposal efforts are worth it. This is sort of connected, but not very strongly.

Now here's why I like this answer choice:

Does a paragraph transition sentence actually NEED to support the main argument of the passage?

If you just look blindly at the answer choices, you might think that B sounds accurate enough to be the answer. But, if you take one step back and think logically for half a second, you can easily see that there's no reason this sentence SHOULD support the main argument. Not every single sentence, taken individually, will support the main idea. Some sentences just get you from one supporting idea to the next supporting idea, and that's perfectly fine.

So, use logic and stuff!!

> **(C)** because it continues the explanation of how acid whey can be disposed of safely.

The sentence in question doesn't talk about HOW acid whey can be disposed of. It just mentions that they might be costly.

(D) because it sets up the argument in the paragraph for the benefits of Greek yogurt.

This it does, for sure. We've discussed repeatedly what the two paragraphs were about and how the bolded sentence transitions between them.

Big Takeaways:

- » Don't look at the "yes/no" or "keep/delete".

- » Use logic. Don't just distance yourself from the passage and blindly read the answer choices.

- » Actually go back to the passage and figure out what the passages are doing and saying. Simple, Ridiculous Summaries can help you for a single paragraph, a long sentence, or even a short clause, in addition to helping you with the whole passage. The SRS is a mentality, not just a single trick. It's the bigger idea of keeping things simply, relaxed, and a bit goofy. It's the mentality of getting to the core of the meaning, not focusing on every single name, date, and detail surrounding the most core idea. Use your SRS mentality!

The article, published by Forbes magazine, explained that coworking spaces are designated locations that, for a fee, individuals can use to conduct their work. The spaces are usually stocked with standard office ㉖ equipment, such as photocopiers, printers, and fax machines. ㉗ In these locations, however, the spaces often include small meeting areas and larger rooms for hosting presentations. ☆ ㉘ **The cost of launching a new coworking business in the United States is estimated to be approximately $58,000.** ☆

What most caught my interest, though, was a quotation from someone who described coworking spaces as "melting pots of creativity." The article refers to a 2012 survey in which ㉙ 64 percent of respondents noted that coworking spaces prevented them from completing tasks in a given time. The article goes on to suggest that the most valuable resources provided by coworking spaces are actually the people ㉚ whom use them.

㉘ The writer is considering deleting the bolded sentence. Should the sentence be kept or deleted?

- **(A)** because it provides a detail that supports the main topic of the paragraph.
- **(B)** because it sets up the main topic of the paragraph that follows.
- **(C)** because it blurs the paragraph's main focus with a loosely related detail.
- **(D)** because it repeats information that has been provided in an earlier paragraph.

Let's ignore the first words here and just focus on disproving three answer choices. Write out your disprovings on paper!

> **(A)** because it provides a detail that supports the main topic of the paragraph

A is wrong because the main idea of the paragraph is that coworking spaces exist and you can use them to work in. The sentence in question tells us how much it would cost if you wanted to start your own business running one of these spaces, but this guy is writing about USING these spaces, not creating them. So, it is a detail, but it doesn't **support** the main topic of the paragraph.

> **(B)** because it sets up the main topic of the paragraph that follows

B is wrong because the next paragraph is about how good (or bad) coworking spaces are at fostering creativity. Again, starting your own coworking space is not at all related.

> **(D)** because it repeats information that has been provided in an earlier paragraph

D is wrong because the sentence in question, we have noted, is a completely different topic from either the paragraph before or the one after. So, it's definitely not repeated information.

> **(C)** because it blurs the paragraph's main focus with a loosely related detail

C is correct. We've gotten at this idea through our discussions of each of the three wrong answers.

So, that's all it takes! But, you have to do it. The number one thing I experience when working with students is this:

- » They come in and say, "It's not working. I got so many questions wrong."
- » We go through the questions they got wrong, and I say, "Did you simplify this? Did you disprove this? Did you think about what it's transitioning from and to? Did you ask yourself questions?"
- » The student sheepishly says, "No…"

You don't have to feel bad about it, though. I'm not judging you. I'm here to guide you to success, and part of your success will come from getting through this hurdle. Judging you isn't going to help you in any way.

Your brain has to take this time to re-program your subconscious, your mental muscle memory, to behave the way that your conscious mind now knows you need to behave. You know you need to simplify things, but your brain is still in American-School-System-Overcomplication Mode. You know you need to disprove things, but your brain still thinks that it should pick the one right answer based on some jumbled up (probably overcomplicated) "evidence". You know you need to ask yourself the right questions to engage your mind, but your brain is biologically programmed to be lazy and not want to.

It's not you; that's just life. That's why you need as much practice as you can possibly squeeze in before your test. You need time to force your brain to behave the way you want it to under pressure. You'll get there.

These days, many ④ student's majoring in philosophy have no intention of becoming philosophers; instead they plan to apply those skills to other disciplines. Law and business specifically benefit from the complicated theoretical issues raised in the study of philosophy, but philosophy can be just as useful in engineering or any field requiring complex analytic skills. ㊷ That these skills are transferable across professions ㊸ which makes them especially beneficial to twenty-first-century students. Because today's students can expect to hold multiple jobs—some of which may not even exist yet—during ㊹ our lifetime, studying philosophy allows them to be flexible and adaptable. High demand, advanced exam scores, and varied professional skills all argue for maintaining and enhancing philosophy courses and majors within academic institutions.

㊷ At this point, the writer is considering adding the following sentence.

The ancient Greek philosopher Plato, for example, wrote many of his works in the form of dialogues.

Should the writer make this addition here?

(A) because it reinforces the passage's main point about the employability of philosophy majors.
(B) because it acknowledges a common counterargument to the passage's central claim.
(C) because it blurs the paragraph's focus by introducing a new idea that goes unexplained.
(D) because it undermines the passage's claim about the employability of philosophy majors.

Again, let's focus on everything after the "because".

205

> **(A)** because it reinforces the passage's main point about the employability of philosophy majors

LOL. Plato was not employed in the modern era. His life, and the way he wrote his works, has pretty much nothing to do with modern employability.

> **(B)** because it acknowledges a common counterargument to the passage's central claim

The central claim of the passage (or from what we've seen anyways) seems to be about how studying Philosophy can be useful for modern day workers. Again, Plato has no real impact on that. Plato certainly isn't a counterargument to the usefulness of Philosophy!

> **(D)** because it undermines the passage's claim about the employability of philosophy majors

This answer choice is pretty useful because it spells out for you what the passage's central claim is… But it's super wrong. Again, Plato doesn't undermine anything about employability of Philosophy peeps.

C is correct. The sentence about Plato would add a new point and then leave it completely undeveloped, unexplained, and confusing.

According to Box, a leading Greenland expert, tundra fires in 2012 from as far away as North America produced great amounts of soot, some ⓘ **of it** drifted over Greenland in giant plumes of smoke and then ⓘ **fell** as particles onto the ice sheet. Scientists have long known that soot particles facilitate melting by darkening snow and ice, limiting ⓘ **it's** ability to reflect the Sun's rays. As Box explains, "Soot is an extremely powerful light absorber. It settles over the ice and captures the Sun's heat." The result is a self-reinforcing cycle. As the ice melts, the land and water under the ice become exposed, and since land and water are darker than snow, the surface absorbs even more heat, which ⓘ **is related to the rising temperatures.**

⓴ Which choice best completes the description of a self-reinforcing cycle?

    (A) NO CHANGE
    (B) raises the surface temperature.
    (C) begins to cool at a certain point.
    (D) leads to additional melting.

Read the question! Take a guess.

Most students, I think, just don't clearly read the question on this one. The question asks you to pick the option that completes a "self-reinforcing cycle". That means that you need to have a clear **cycle** or loop by the end of the sentence.

As the ice melts, the land and water under the ice become exposed, and since land and water are darker than snow, the surface absorbs even more heat, which _____.

Step 1: The ice melts. (Step 1 must also be the final step, in order to create a **cycle**.)
Step 2: Land and water under the ice are exposed.
Step 3: Land and water absorb even more heat (because they are darker).
Step 4 (and final): The ice melts some more. (This must be the case in order to create a cycle.)

Steps 1 and 4 are the same, and thus it is a cycle. It's self-reinforcing because the more the ice melts, the more heat gets absorbed (and then even more ice will melt causing even more heat to get absorbed, etc.). So, the answer is D.

You know what a cycle is. You know what a loop is. And yet, many students still get this one wrong. Again, make sure you're talking to yourself through these questions. Ask yourself, "What does a self-reinforcing cycle look like?" Or just, "What does a cycle look like?" Stay engaged and you'll get questions like this.

Because philosophy ㊱ teaching students not what to think but how to think, the age-old discipline offers consistently useful tools for academic and professional achievement. ㊲ A 1994 survey concluded that only 18 percent of American colleges required at least one philosophy course. ㊳ Therefore, between 1992 and 1996, more than 400 independent philosophy departments were eliminated from institutions.

㊲ Which choice most effectively sets up the information that follows?

(A) Consequently, philosophy students have been receiving an increasing number of job offers.
(B) Therefore, because of the evidence, colleges increased their offerings in philosophy.
(C) Notwithstanding the attractiveness of this course of study, students have resisted majoring in philosophy.
(D) However, despite its many utilitarian benefits, colleges have not always supported the study of philosophy.

This one is a great candidate for "What would it look like?"

(A) Consequently, philosophy students have been receiving an increasing number of job offers.

If it were A, then the next sentences would need to talk about job offers and increases.

(B) Therefore, because of the evidence, colleges increased their offerings in philosophy.

If it were B, then we'd need to see increases in the number of philosophy classes, professors, majors, minors, something.

(C) Notwithstanding the attractiveness of this course of study, students have resisted majoring in philosophy.

If it were C, we'd need to see some decreases in the numbers of philosophy majors and a discussion of why students didn't like philosophy enough to major in it. (This one is pretty contrary to the entire passage, so hopefully you didn't pick this.)

We don't see any of the things above. The next several sentences tell us that colleges are taking away philosophy programs, which is exactly what D is saying: "colleges have not always supported the study of philosophy".

Key Takeaways for these question types:

» Read. In the grammar section, focus on your reading skills. If you read well, it will carry you through several grammar questions as well. If you read poorly, you have no hope of a good score.

» Keep things simple! I cannot say this enough times. In fact, I could probably write a 300 page book in which all I do is write "Keep it simple!" several thousand times, and that would be a useful tool for your SAT study. You have been brainwashed for years into believing that if it's not complicated, then it's not smart. You have to UNbrainwash yourself, and that's going to take time and commitment.

» Take a step back and use logic. Don't get so stuck in the details all the time. Details can help as a tiebreaker. Details are good when you're not sure how to disprove something. But, a lot of times, all you need to do is think about the logical likelihood of something, or the simple realities of the world. Remember to stay grounded during these tests!

Transition Word Questions

Next, I want to get into Transition Word questions. For some strange reason, students generally really struggle with these questions. So, I want to reframe this skill for you, simply.

You already know what all of these words do. You just have to ask yourself the questions.

Answer the following on a piece of paper:

1. When do you use these words: consequently, therefore, accordingly, hence, thus

2. When do you use these words: furthermore, in addition, moreover, in fact

3. When do you use these words: similarly, also, likewise

4. When do you use these words: although, but, conversely, even so, however, in contrast, nevertheless, nonetheless, notwithstanding, otherwise, still, yet

5. When do you use these words: for example, for instance, specifically, that is, to illustrate

Answers

1. When you want to show **Cause and Effect**.
2. When you want to provide **More** information.
3. When you want to **Compare**.
4. When you want to **Contrast**.
5. When you want to give an **Example**.

Like I said, none of that is complicated. Now, you just have to always ask yourself which of those five the sentence(s) are getting at.

❻ Though these conservation methods can be costly and time-consuming, they are well worth the effort. Nutritionists consider Greek yogurt to be a healthy food: it is an excellent source of calcium and protein, serves ❼ to be a digestive aid, and ❽ it contains few calories in its unsweetened low- and non-fat forms. Greek yogurt is slightly lower in sugar and carbohydrates than conventional yogurt is.

✶ ❾ Also, ✶ because it is more concentrated, Greek yogurt contains slightly more protein per serving, thereby helping people stay ❿ satiated for longer periods of time. These health benefits have prompted Greek yogurt's recent surge in popularity. In fact, Greek yogurt can be found in an increasing number of products such as snack food and frozen desserts. Because consumers reap the nutritional benefits of Greek yogurt and support those who make and sell ⓫ it, therefore farmers and businesses should continue finding safe and effective methods of producing the food.

❾

- (A) NO CHANGE
- (B) In other words,
- (C) Therefore,
- (D) For instance,

So, our options are:

- (A) More of the same
- (B) Restating the same
    ("in other words" has to be a direct rephrasing of the same idea)
- (C) Cause/Effect
- (D) Example

Find your answer!

Answer is A.

There is no Cause or Effect and no Example of anything. This paragraph is just a big long list of a bunch of great things about Greek yogurt and how it's healthy and stuff. So, a lot of the Same.

But! It's not a direct restating of the prior sentence, so it can't be B.

Typically, the ice sheet begins to show evidence of thawing in late ⑬ summer. This follows several weeks of higher temperatures.

⑭ **For example,** in the summer of 2012, virtually the entire Greenland Ice Sheet underwent thawing at or near its surface by mid-July, the earliest date on record. Most scientists looking for the causes of the Great Melt of 2012 have focused exclusively on rising temperatures. The summer of 2012 was the warmest in 170 years, records show. But Jason ⑮ Box, an associate professor of geology at Ohio State believes that another factor added to the early ⑯ thaw; the "dark snow" problem.

⑭

- (A) NO CHANGE
- (B) However,
- (C) As such,
- (D) Moreover,

So, our options are:

- (A) Example
- (B) Contrast
- (C) Cause/Effect
- (D) More of the same

Pick your answer!

217

It's definitely not a Cause/Effect situation, and it's not more of the same information. The second sentence is far more specific, which suggests either a Compare/Contrast thing or an Example.

Most students get this one wrong, and they pick For example.

Reread the question and see if you can find evidence proving that the second sentence is NOT an example of the first sentence.

Two things:

First, it says that this one instance was "the earliest date on record". That would be different from the norm, for sure. Not an example of the norm.

Second, the first sentence says that "typically, the ice sheet begins to show evidence of thawing in **late summer**." But, the next sentence says that in 2012, Greenland was melting by **mid-July**.

Most students just aren't very precise with their concept of time, and they assume that "mid-July" sort of counts as "late summer". It does not. July is the middle of the summer. The summer is colloquially considered to be June, July, and August. July would be the middle month. Mid-July would be the middle of the middle month…very definitionally not "late" summer.

But also, many students just aren't reading closely enough to see small words like "late" in the Grammar section. The Grammar section is about Grammar, right?! We don't have to focus on every word… right?!

Wrong. The Grammar section is about one third reading comprehension. So, pay attention to the details that you would normally use to disprove. If you're struggling with the Reading section of the SAT as well, then study both Reading and Grammar simultaneously. They will reinforce each other, and you'll come out stronger and victorious!

The article, published by Forbes magazine, explained that coworking spaces are designated locations that, for a fee, individuals can use to conduct their work. The spaces are usually stocked with standard office ㉖ equipment, such as photocopiers, printers, and fax machines. ㉗ **In these locations, however,** the spaces often include small meeting areas and larger rooms for hosting presentations. ㉘ The cost of launching a new coworking business in the United States is estimated to be approximately $58,000.

㉗

(A) NO CHANGE
(B) In addition to equipment,
(C) For these reasons,
(D) Likewise,

Write out the four options you have here (Example, Cause/Effect, More, etc.) and figure it out.

221

Your options here are:

- **(A)** Contrast
- **(B)** More of the same
- **(C)** Cause/Effect
- **(D)** More of the same

And here your SAT-Guessing-Method nonsense tells you that it cannot be either B or D because they're sort of the same.

DO NOT do SAT Guessing Method nonsense!!!

If you did that, let's all take a moment to laugh at you a bit. Ahahahaahhaa. Teeheehee. Lol.

Mk, now, it's no biggie if you did think that. Actually, it's perfect. It means that you needed to take this exact moment to laugh about the SAT Guessing Method and get on the path towards not using it ever again.

Next, you should have asked yourself, "What is the passage doing? Compare/Contrast? Cause/Effect? Elaboration?"

The sentence just prior talks about things that coworking spaces have. The sentence in question talks about...things that coworking spaces have. So, we know it MUST BE either B or D!

What's the difference? You tell me. Think about it for a second. Engage with whatever you know. Try to explain and write down the difference between "in addition to" and "likewise".

In addition to is like:

In addition to all this XXX, there is also this YYY.

Likewise is like:

This XXX is this way. Likewise, this YYY is the same way.

So, you could think of it as "likewise" being essentially "like ways" or "in the same way"

Which of those two is happening in this question?

The first.

Long viewed by many as the stereotypical useless major, philosophy is now being seen by many students and prospective employers as in fact a very useful and practical major, offering students a host of transferable skills with relevance to the modern workplace. **34 In broad terms,** philosophy is the study of meaning and the values underlying thought and behavior. But 35 more pragmatically, the discipline encourages students to analyze complex material, question conventional beliefs, and express thoughts in a concise manner.

34

(A) NO CHANGE
(B) For example,
(C) In contrast,
(D) Nevertheless,

Think about what these four options are. Then, figure out your answer!

225

Your options are:

- **(A)** Literally just "here is some general/broad information" (Sometimes there are less common transitional words and phrases that don't fit the common 5 categories.)
- **(B)** Example
- **(C)** Contrast
- **(D)** Contrast, but specifically showing a better side of something (some distinctly positive information should follow this word)

Then, you ask yourself what the previous sentence was about. Is the sentence in question an example or a contrasting piece of information…?

No. It's just a generic description of philosophy. So, A is good!

Because philosophy ㊱ teaching students not what to think but how to think, the age-old discipline offers consistently useful tools for academic and professional achievement. ㊲ However, despite its many utilitarian benefits, colleges have not always supported the study of philosophy. ㊳ **Therefore,** between 1992 and 1996, more than 400 independent philosophy departments were eliminated from institutions.

㊳

(A) NO CHANGE
(B) Thus,
(C) Moreover,
(D) However,

Think it out!

Our options are:

- **(A)** Cause/Effect
- **(B)** Also Cause/Effect
- **(C)** More Info
- **(D)** Contrast

We're not looking at cause and effect or contrast here. The sentence prior is saying that colleges don't care about philosophy. This sentence talks about colleges ditching philosophy classes and departments and stuff. Those two things are totally in line with each other. One is just More information about the same thing.

Answer is C.

I will note that, on the real test, this question is made much harder by the fact that question 36 had you change the entire preceding sentence! So, if you got 37 wrong, you'd almost certainly get 38 wrong as well.

Even if you were to get 37 correct, you'd still be looking at the original, wrong sentence written in the passage while looking at question 38. You'd have to remind yourself to think about the correct sentence, not the one in front of you...

Remember, the SAT is a tricky little trickster. They're trying to trap you and trick you at every turn. Your job, with this book as help, is to learn their tricks and beat them at their own game. You can do it. You already have 90% of the skills within you. I'm here to unlock those skills and teach you the remaining 10%.

Key Takeaways for Transition Words

- » You MUST ask yourself what you're transitioning From and To with the sentence prior and after.
- » There are only a few main things to look for:
  - Cause/Effect
  - More Information
  - Compare or Contrast
  - Example
- » If you actually think it through, you'll get these questions correct. If you're still getting a lot of Transition Word Questions wrong, then you just aren't yet committing to asking yourself the questions and picking out which of those 4 things is happening.

It's as simple as that.

A few years ago, my brother and I went sky diving. We had to go tandem, which means we were attached to an experienced jumper who did all the parachute stuff. We were just along for the ride.

When we were preparing to go up there, the guys told us one of the best pieces of advice I'd ever heard:

If you can't breathe, it's because you're not breathing.

They told us that many people get up there, in the air, just jumped out of a plane, and they think they can't breathe. They genuinely panic, and some of them even pass out. But, there is absolutely nothing, at that height, that would prevent them from breathing.

If you can't breathe...it's simply because you aren't breathing.

In much the same way, if you can't get some particular type of question right, it's just because you aren't doing the steps. It's not because you actually can't. It's because your brain has gone into panic mode and has abandoned all rational thought, all the rules, tips, and tricks, all of it.

Remember, that's okay. It's just a thing to work through. Now is the time to work through it. THIS is what practice tests are for. They're not just for suffering through and getting one abysmal score after another. They're for progressive improvements, tweaks, changes, and reinforcements (of the skills that matter most!).

Charts

Remember all that Reading up in this Grammar section? Well, now it's time for...Math. Ya, not Grammar. It's math time.

Remember, the SAT is trying to trick you. There is grammar in the reading, reading in the math, math in the grammar, and everything else. Don't put up blinders and pretend that your other skills don't exist suddenly just because you're in one section or another.

To be fair, though, this is just reading a chart... It's not exactly math. But, you get my point.

Most of Greenland's interior is covered by a thick layer of ice and compressed snow known as the Greenland Ice Sheet. The size of the ice sheet fluctuates seasonally: in summer, average daily high temperatures in Greenland can rise to slightly above 50 degrees Fahrenheit, partially melting the ice; in the winter, the sheet thickens as additional snow falls, and average daily low temperatures can drop **12 to as low as 20 degrees.**

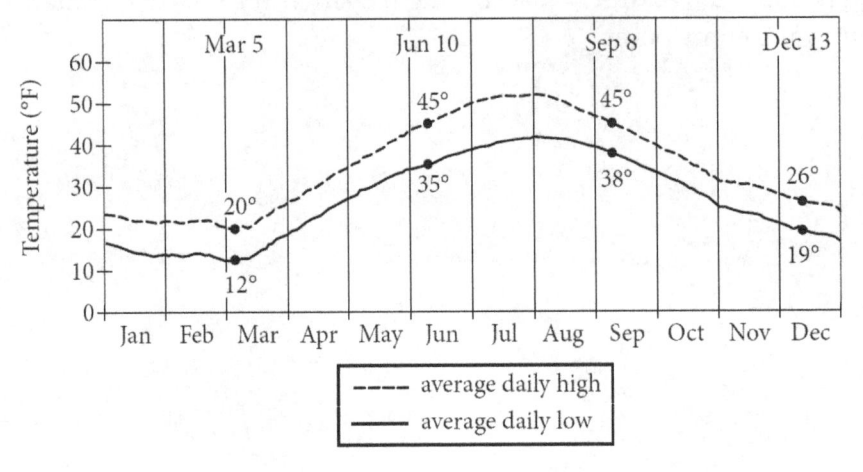

Average Daily High and Low Temperatures Recorded at Nuuk Weather Station, Greenland (1961–1990)

Adapted from WMO. ©2014 by World Meteorological Organization.

12 Which choice most accurately and effectively represents the information in the graph?

(A) NO CHANGE
(B) to 12 degrees Fahrenheit.
(C) to their lowest point on December 13.
(D) to 10 degrees Fahrenheit and stay there for months.

If you only look at the graph, only one of the answers is at all true. This isn't a grammar question by any means at all. A says "to as low as 20 degrees", but the temperatures get lower than that. C says "to their lowest point on December 13", but the graph continues downwards after Dec 13. D says "to 10 degrees Fahrenheit and stay there for months", but the graph doesn't ever reach that low at all.

The answer is B. You just have to look at the graph.

This is, by the way, also true for the reading section most of the time. The reading section will often ask questions about the graphs and charts, and only one answer will even be accurate for the charts. This saves you time because you don't have to go review the passage; you can look solely at the chart or graph.

The main instance when this is not true is when the question says something like, "Which of the following statements from the graph is supported by the passage." Then, usually, all four will be supported by the graph, but only one will be true in the passage.

Anyways, that's enough of a digression into reading. On with the math inside of grammar! lol

What most caught my interest, though, was a quotation from someone who described coworking spaces as "melting pots of creativity." The article refers to a 2012 survey in which ⭐ **㉙ 64 percent of respondents noted that coworking spaces prevented them from completing tasks in a given time.** ⭐ The article goes on to suggest that the most valuable resources provided by coworking spaces are actually the people ㉚ <u>whom use</u> them.

㉙ At this point, the writer wants to add specific information that supports the main topic of the paragraph.

Perceived Effect of Coworking on Business Skills

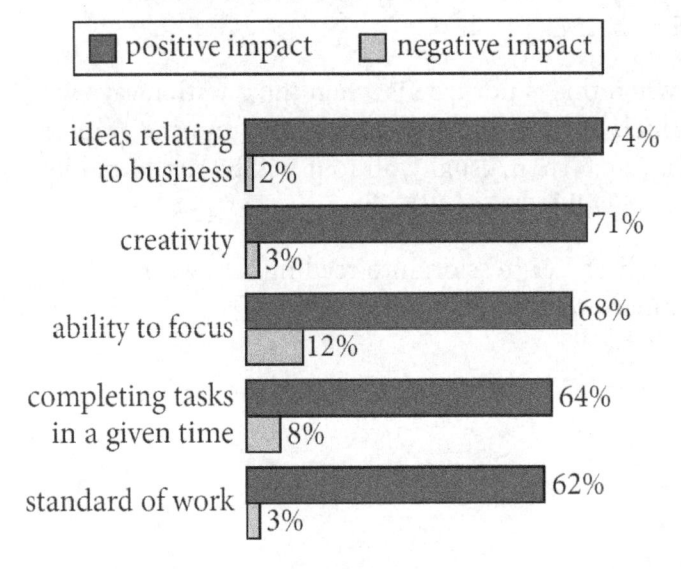

■ positive impact   ■ negative impact

- ideas relating to business: 74% / 2%
- creativity: 71% / 3%
- ability to focus: 68% / 12%
- completing tasks in a given time: 64% / 8%
- standard of work: 62% / 3%

Adapted from "The 3rd Global Coworking Survey." ©2013 by Deskmag.

Which choice most effectively completes the sentence with relevant and accurate information based on the graph above?

(A) NO CHANGE
(B) 71 percent of respondents indicated that using a coworking space increased their creativity.
(C) respondents credited coworking spaces with giving them 74 percent of their ideas relating to business.
(D) respondents revealed that their ability to focus on their work improved by 12 percent in a coworking space.

Take a guess, first.

Now, this question is a great place to review what the given information is actually telling us. Answer the following questions.

1. What is the title of this chart?
2. What do the darker bars tell us?
3. What does the 12% on "ability to focus" mean?

Answers

1. The title of this chart is "Perceived Effect of Coworking on Business Skills". Translation: How do people think coworking spaces impacted them?
2. They tell us the percentage of people who stated they got a positive impact in each of those categories. That means that it does NOT tell us how much of an impact people experienced, how much things improved, etc. It's just a percentage of people who felt one way or another.
3. It means that 12% of people surveyed claimed to experience a negative impact on their ability to focus. Note that all surveys have no guarantee of truth; they are just what people say. That is one very big limitation on the types of conclusions we can draw from such data, and it is why the title of the chart is **Perceived** effect...

At this point, feel free to take a second guess.

Based on the above, we can see that C and D are completely false. The respondents were not asked **how many** of their business ideas came from the coworking space. They were simply asked if the coworking space had a positive or negative impact on stuff. Furthermore, the survey didn't ask **how much** their ability to focus improved (or didn't). So, that 12% doesn't give us an amount of improvement.

A is just backwards. 64% said it helped, not hurt, them.

And, indeed, 71% of the people said the coworking space had a positive impact on their creativity. So, B is our answer.

We won't do a ton of these together, but here are the big takeaways:

» On the grammar section, you will need to read critically and analyze mathematical data in charts. It is NOT a purely grammar section.

» For graphs, always ask yourself what the title is (and then answer yourself).

» Always figure out what **one** data point means. Once you read over the graph, you can say, "Okay, so then this 78 over here means _____." It'll only take you a second, and it will help to fight against misreading due to rushing or your brain checking out (because brains are annoying and not always good teammates).

That's all! Proceed.

Vocabulary Questions

Vocabulary questions break down in two ways:

1. You either know it or you don't.
2. You can reason through it based on context (though most of you aren't yet very skilled at this).

So, guess what... It's time for more Vocab Synapse lectures!

DO YOUR VOCAB SYNAPSE!

Seriously, you won't regret it. Students never come and tell me they regret doing it, even when the exact words they see don't show up on their tests (though a few always do, if you practice enough). Remember, our Vocab Synapse program also teaches you word contexts, synonyms, and Latin roots. You will use those exact skills to get the vocabulary questions on the SAT Reading and Grammar sections correct.

Last thing here: Remember that you cannot "reason" your way through a complex vocab word with no clear roots. When you hit a question that is "know it or not", you need to know it. So, do your Synapse!

Set up a free consultation with us today at www.VohraMethod.com and we'll get you set up with it completely for free.

Greek yogurt—a strained form of cultured yogurt—has grown enormously in popularity in the United States since it was first introduced in the country in the late 1980s.

From 2011 to 2012 alone, sales of Greek yogurt in the US increased by 50 percent. The resulting increase in Greek yogurt production has forced those involved in the business to address the detrimental effects that the yogurt-making process may be having on the environment. Fortunately, farmers and others in the Greek yogurt business have found many methods of controlling and eliminating most environmental threats. Given these solutions as well as the many health benefits of the food, the advantages of Greek yogurt ❶ **outdo** the potential drawbacks of its production.

❶

    (A) NO CHANGE
    (B) defeat
    (C) outperform
    (D) outweigh

Take a guess, then we'll discuss.

The best way for most students to attack these questions, I find, is to ask yourself, "What is the usual context of this word?"

What is the usual context of the following words? (In other words, where do I usually see these words? In art? Sports? Law? Politics? In a scientific journal or an opinion article? On Insta or the Library of Congress? Etc.)

Just think of the most common places you might have seen these words. Go with what you know; don't look for overly complex contexts that you don't know very well.

- **(A)** Outdo
- **(B)** Defeat
- **(C)** Outperform
- **(D)** Outweigh

Answers

1. Outdo is usually used in a competitive situation. You might outdo your opponent. You might also outdo yourself (if you break your own personal best record or something). You might have heard the phrase, "You've outdone yourself." That can also apply when you do something above and beyond for someone, usually a gift (physical or something you did for them).

2. Defeat is definitely sports, competition, war, fighting, politics, debate, etc.

3. Outperform is also usually a competition thing. It makes me think more of gymnastics and other performance-based Olympic games. Maybe dance. Anything with performances. I also know (you may or may not) that people use "outperform" in the world of marketing where one product can outperform another on the marketplace. That just means that more people buy it in comparison to the other product.

4. Outweigh is used whenever you're weighing options and one of them seems better. It's not quite competitive. It's more like if you're deciding between Vanilla or Mint Chocolate Chip, and you just got new braces. You decide not to go with choco chips, because they might hurt your teeth. It's just a weighing of options.

Now, one more question. What is the thing that is outdoing/defeating/outperforming/outweighing the other thing? Look for the big nouns on either side of the word. Two things are being compared here.

5. The _____ is/are outdoing/defeating/outperforming/outweighing the _____.

5. The **advantages** are outdoing/defeating/outperforming/outweighing the **disadvantages**.

   Are the advantages in a direct competition, war, fight? No. A, B, and C are very oriented around competing and fighting. D is just about weighing options, weighing positives and negatives (or advantages and disadvantages…).

   Answer is D.

❻ Though these conservation methods can be costly and time-consuming, they are well worth the effort. Nutritionists consider Greek yogurt to be a healthy food: it is an excellent source of calcium and protein, serves ❼ to be a digestive aid, and ❽ it contains few calories in its unsweetened low- and non-fat forms. Greek yogurt is slightly lower in sugar and carbohydrates than conventional yogurt is. ❾ Also, because it is more concentrated, Greek yogurt contains slightly more protein per serving, thereby helping people stay ❿ **satiated** for longer periods of time. These health benefits have prompted Greek yogurt's recent surge in popularity. In fact, Greek yogurt can be found in an increasing number of products such as snack food and frozen desserts. Because consumers reap the nutritional benefits of Greek yogurt and support those who make and sell ⓫ it, therefore farmers and businesses should continue finding safe and effective methods of producing the food.

❿

- (A) NO CHANGE
- (B) fulfilled
- (C) complacent
- (D) sufficient

What is the context for each word? Write it all down, then take your guess!

1. Satiated
2. Fulfilled
3. Complacent
4. Sufficient

Answers

1. Satiated is used to talk about food and feeling full.

2. Fulfilled is usually used to talk about your life and its meaning and if you feel generally satisfied with how your life is going. (This is a bit of a trick answer because it has the sounds "full" and "fill" in it, both of which are associated with food. But, this word isn't about food usually.) This is not a contextual match.

3. Complacent is also more of a general life thing. If you're pleased with yourself and how things are, you're complacent (though with this word, there's usually some bad thing that you're unaware of coming your way). This one is wrong because it isn't a definitional match.

4. Sufficient just means enough. It is used all over the place: sufficient training for the SAT, sufficient practice for the big game, sufficient knowledge for the task, sufficient food for the journey. But, things don't usually cause people to "stay sufficient" or "stay at the just enough mark".

The context of the sentence in question is about feeling full. The answer is A. If you knew Satiated, then this question was easy. If you did not know the word Satiated, you could still disprove the three other, more common words by thinking about their usual contexts! So, don't despair if you don't know a particular vocab word. Just rely on your trusty skills of disproving.

I liked the experience so much that I now go to the coworking space a few times a week. Over time, I've gotten to know several of my coworking ③② colleagues: another website developer, a graphic designer, a freelance writer, and several mobile app coders. Even those of us who work in disparate fields are able to ③③ **share advice** and help each other brainstorm. In fact, it's the diversity of their talents and experiences that makes my coworking colleagues so valuable.

③③

    (A) NO CHANGE
    (B) give some wisdom
    (C) proclaim our opinions
    (D) opine

Think about contexts, answer the following, then take a guess.

    1. When does someone give wisdom?

    2. When does someone proclaim his/her opinions?

    3. When does someone opine?

Answers

1. Maybe a grandparent or parent might share some wisdom with you (if they are wise…). Friends can share wisdom with each other when they are dealing with a difficult problem.

2. If they are giving a speech. Definitely in politics. Maybe in a smaller group? But proclaim is usually a big thing to a lot of people.

3. Opine just means to have or state an opinion about a thing. It's not the same as sharing advice that would help someone else. When you don't know words here, you should be looking them up and creating flash cards. Physical, digital, I don't care. Just make them and practice them in addition to your Vocab Synapse. There are some words the SAT really likes to use a lot, so study those.

So, these people are probably not proclaiming or going on at length about their opinions. They're just helpfully trying to share ideas. So, is it A or B?

It's A, share advice. They could, theoretically, share wisdom OR advice. But, the phrase "give some wisdom" is just the weirdest way of saying it. We would generally say "share wisdom with [person]". B is wrong because it's clunky and weirdly phrased. That's a useful thing to look out for, though it is harder to spot if you're not a **big reader**.

If you are, then "share some wisdom" sounds weird to you, and you could theoretically answer this based on "sound". But, the vast majority of you guys are used to hearing English spoken by…your peers. And, no offense, but that isn't generally the best measuring stick, you know? So, don't do the SAT based on "sound". It doesn't work.

That's all for vocab for now. These are just example problems; they aren't meant to be exhaustive. The goal of this phase is to get you thinking, get you to start seeing the skills needed and making the connections that will reinforce those skills.

Takeaways for Vocab:

- DO YOUR VOCAB SYNAPSE for 20+ minutes per day.

- Whenever you see ANY word you don't know ANYwhere in the world, look up the definition and make yourself a flashcard. Every complex word you find in SAT practice tests (in reading, grammar, or math), every word you don't know in a book you're reading for fun, even words you don't know in books and articles you're being forced to read and actually hate them, all of those words…look them up. Every time.

- Practice thinking about contexts for the vocab answer choices. This is a useful skill that can turn a "don't know it" moment into a success.

Test 2

Next, you're going to take Test 2. Test 2 is no longer listed on the College Board's website. You can find it here: www.VohraMethod.com/crash-course-resources

For this test, you'll try an experiment. This helps some students, but not all. It's worth testing out!

Experiment: Read through this test and try to write down which skill is being tested for each question. You can use whatever shorthand you'd like. If you're not sure, that's fine. Just try to figure out what skill is being tested (or sometimes multiple skills) before picking your answer.

I'll make a full list of the skills tested in each question, and then we'll dive into some of the questions that are generally more challenging.

Remember, if you're having a lot of trouble with a particular question type, you can always come meet with me for an hour. You can get in touch at www.VohraMethod.com/crash-course-resources.

So, take the test, list out the skills, and write down your answers!

Skills List

1. Subject, Verb, Direct Object kind of thing. (It's not about Verb Conjugations.)
2. Transition Words
3. Subject-Verb Agreement
4. Critical Reading – Adding Information
5. Brevity & a bit of common usage/phrasing
6. Parallel Structure
7. Redundancy, Critical Reading
8. Joining Clauses, Independent vs Dependent Clauses
9. Redundancy
10. Parallel Structure (with similar tone) & Brevity
11. Critical Reading
12. Transition Words
13. Commas
14. Colons
15. Critical Reading – Adding Information
16. More of a Disprove; Don't Prove question. Comma Splice is bad. Redundancy is bad. Sentence Fragments are bad. (Answer choice C is good!)
17. Critical Reading & a bit of Redundancy

18. Process of elimination & a weird Colons thing

19. Parallel Structure

20. Possessives, Plural vs Singular

21. Dangling Modifier

22. Critical Reading – Paragraph Ordering

23. Mostly Clauses (making sure that all clauses have a subject & verb, even modifying clauses)

24. Chart Reading

25. Transition Words

26. Critical Reading – Adding Information

27. Commas (also looking at the context to see there are no other dashes or quote marks)

28. Vocabulary in Context

29. Pronoun-Antecedent Agreement

30. Pronoun-Antecedent Agreement + the antecedent needs to have been mentioned recently enough.

31. Critical Reading – Adding Information and Sentence Ordering

32. Critical Reading – Context

33. Commas (appositives)

34. Just a weird one

35. Punctuation (commas, semicolons, dashes)

36. Vocabulary

37. Critical Reading

38. Then vs Than

39. Verb tense (and avoiding comma splice)

40. Transition Words

41. Verb Tense + Vocabulary (await vs. wait)

42. Critical Reading – Sentence Ordering

43. Critical Reading – Adding Information

44. Transition Words

So! You can see what's more and less common. Once you grade your answers, you should review any skills that you're still getting wrong. By review, I don't mean look at the question, look at the right answer, tell yourself you understand why that one is the right answer, and then move on. That is nonsense. That is nothing at all. That is not going to get you any score increase of any kind, I guarantee it.

When I say review, I mean that you should go back to the section of this book that dealt with that topic and reread everything in that section. Redo all the practice problems in that section. If you're still getting some of those wrong, you can look for more practice problems online. (You have the skill name, so just search "[skill name] practice problems".) If all that isn't enough, or if you still don't fully, completely understand the topic, then come and meet with me, or talk to a knowledgeable English teacher at your school. Just remember, they will likely try to overcomplicate things. If you get an overcomplicated answer from your teacher, then don't go back to that teacher.

Any truly smart person can explain the most advanced topics to a 5-year-old. Everything in the world can be explained simply and clearly. Nothing needs to be so complex it gives you a headache. Nothing.

Conquering these skills will require a combination of recognizing what skill is being tested, and then knowing how to correctly apply that skill (or several skills). Work on both of those things. Test your knowledge of the skill being tested in each grammar question, and then test your knowledge at applying the skill!

Below, I'll review the Critical Reading questions and a few other questions that I think are worthy of note. Anything I don't review below, be sure to fully review on your own.

As a reminder, that means:

1. See what skill was being tested.

2. Reread the section of this book that talks about that skill.

3. Redo the practice problems for that skill.

4. Come back to the Test 2 question and take a second guess. (This means that you cannot write down the correct answer on your test page or answer page. You need to be able to genuinely give it a second guess. Not just look at the answer and convince yourself that you know why that answer is correct!!)

5. If you ever feel really stuck, set up a meeting with me at www.vohramethod.com/crash-course-resources. Grammar is usually the quickest portion of the test to conquer!

Reviewing Select Questions from Test 2

The share of library materials that is in nonprint formats is increasing steadily; in 2010, at least 18.5 million e-books were available ★ ❺ **for them to circulate.** ★

❺

    (A) NO CHANGE
    (B) to be circulated by them.
    (C) for their circulating.
    (D) for circulation.

This one is D.

Brevity is a big one here, but also…Who is "them"?

The plural nouns in this sentence are mainly inside of modifiers. "materials", "formats". There are also "e-books". Are any of those plural nouns "them"?

Nope. There is no "them" in this sentence, which disproves A, B, and C. If you didn't think of that when you took the test, no worries. Now you've been exposed to a new way of seeing problems, a new detail worth noticing!

Since one of the fastest growing library services is public access computer use, there is great demand for computer instruction. **❼ In fact, librarians' training now includes courses on research and Internet search methods. Many of whom teach classes in Internet navigation, database and software use, and digital information literacy.**

❼ Which choice most effectively combines the underlined sentences?

(A) In fact, librarians' training now includes courses on research and Internet search methods; many librarians teach classes in Internet navigation, database and software use, and digital information literacy is taught by them.

(B) In fact, many librarians, whose training now includes courses on research and Internet search methods, teach classes in Internet navigation, database and software use, and digital information literacy.

(C) Training now includes courses on research and Internet search methods; many librarians, in fact, are teaching classes in Internet navigation, database and software use, and digital information literacy.

(D) Including courses on research and Internet search methods in their training is, in fact, why many librarians teach classes in Internet navigation, database and software use, and digital information literacy.

A has redundancy. "teach classes in" and "is taught by them".

B is correct.

Most students don't pick C. It's clunky and weird phrasing, and it abruptly shifts from the previous sentence about the need for computer instruction to some kind of training. The training is the sub-point.

The main point of the sentence is the courses that librarians offer, not those that they take.

D doesn't make any logical sense. They don't teach classes **because** they are trained in things. They would select training based on whatever classes they're planning to offer.

While these classes are particularly helpful to young students developing basic research skills, **❽ but** adult patrons can also benefit from librarian assistance in that they can acquire job-relevant computer skills.

❽

(A) NO CHANGE
(B) and
(C) for
(D) DELETE the underlined portion.

{comma} BUT joins two independent clauses.

So do {comma} AND and {comma} FOR.

The first clause is dependent. It is an adverb clause modifying "can also benefit".

Answer is D. Always be on the lookout for Independent vs Dependent Clauses when you see any punctuation questions, joining sentences questions, etc.

❾ Free to all who utilize their services, public libraries and librarians are especially valuable, because they offer free resources that may be difficult to find elsewhere, such as help with online job searches as well as résumé and job material development.

❾ Which choice most effectively sets up the examples given at the end of the sentence?

(A) NO CHANGE
(B) During periods of economic recession,
(C) Although their value cannot be measured,
(D) When it comes to the free services libraries provide,

This one is just pure Redundancy. It's a great example of it!

A and D repeat the concept of "free" resources and services mentioned later in the sentence.

C mentions not being able to measure value...and then the rest of the sentence talks about how "especially valuable" libraries are. So, that is more contradictory, not redundant.

B is correct!

In sum, the Internet does not replace the need for librarians, and librarians are hardly obsolete. **⑪ Like books, librarians have been around for a long time, but the Internet is extremely useful for many types of research.**

⑪ Which choice most clearly ends the passage with a restatement of the writer's primary claim?

(A) NO CHANGE
(B) Although their roles have diminished significantly, librarians will continue to be employed by public libraries for the foreseeable future.
(C) The growth of electronic information has led to a diversification of librarians' skills and services, positioning them as savvy resource specialists for patrons.
(D) However, given their extensive training and skills, librarians who have been displaced by budget cuts have many other possible avenues of employment.

Did you stop to ask yourself "What is the writer's primary claim?"

If you did, way to crush it!

If you didn't, think of how silly your brain is sometimes! The question is asking about something related to a primary claim, and your brain is up in here like, "I can totally do this! I don't need to know what the primary claim even is!!"

That kind of bizarre braggadocio is going to get you a mediocre (or abysmal) SAT score. So, give your brain a stern talking to and then change.

But, change doesn't happen immediately. Try as we might, our brains often don't do what we want them to…at least not at first. **You need 10+ practice tests before your real SAT because you need to take that time to get the exact same type of question wrong 3 or 4 times and really get to that breaking point of just, "OH MY GOSH BRAIN!!**

I TOLD you to do the thing. You STILL aren't doing the thing. COME ON!!"

And then, when you're really dedicated to the change and you really yell at your brain…your brain will begrudgingly fall in line.

I like to tell my students to find new and creative ways to torture their brains. I know it sounds crazy (most of my methods sound at least a little ridiculous), but it works.

Brains are lazy, right? So, if you say, "Okay brain, you have two choices. You can either remember this information or skill or tactic (etc.) OR I will sit down and copy the information down 100 times!!"

Next, your brain will call your bluff. It won't remember the thing, and you'll have to actually copy it down 100 times.

But THEN we're in business. Then, your brain thinks, "Oh gosh. This did not go the way I thought… I really want to be lazy, and this kid is forcing me to read and write these same words hundreds of times! Yikes!"

And then, usually, your brain will remember the information. If it doesn't, then copy it down 200 times, or 300. Or do flashcards for 20 minutes, then 40, then an hour per day. Or write a little song/jingle to help you memorize the information (if it's a pure memory thing) and then sing yourself that jingle 100 times per day.

Whatever you do, make it SO HARD and SO LABORIOUS for your brain to avoid remembering the information…that your brain just caves and does the learning and remembering you want it to.

All of this is part of the process, and it takes time. It doesn't take forever, so don't go panicking about time like a weirdo. But it does take some time, so you need to allocate the time you need to get your brain in shape for the big day.

~Now, what is the author's primary claim?

Primary Claim: This passage is basically about how librarians are still important and stuff, even with the internet. Actually, the internet gave them new jobs like…teaching how to use the internet! And also job services and whatever.

- **(A)** NO CHANGE (Like books, librarians have been around for a long time, but the Internet is extremely useful for many types of research.)
- **(B)** Although their roles have diminished significantly, librarians will continue to be employed by public libraries for the foreseeable future.
- **(C)** The growth of electronic information has led to a diversification of librarians' skills and services, positioning them as savvy resource specialists for patrons.
- **(D)** However, given their extensive training and skills, librarians who have been displaced by budget cuts have many other possible avenues of employment.

The passage is NOT about how long librarians have been around. Nor is it about what librarians will do after they get fired, or how long they will likely stay employed.

C is the answer. This is SRS plain and simple. If you have a good SRS, you'll always be in a stronger position on the test.

Viewing the exhibit, I was amazed by the intricate details of some of the more ornately decorated rooms. I marveled at a replica of a salon (a formal living room) dating back to the reign of French king Louis XV. ★ **15** ★ Built into the dark paneled walls are bookshelves stocked with leather-bound volumes. The couch and chairs, in keeping with the style of the time, are characterized by elegantly curved arms and legs and are covered in luxurious velvet. A dime-sized portrait of a French aristocratic woman hangs in a golden frame.

15 At this point, the writer is considering adding the following sentence.

Some scholars argue that the excesses of King Louis XV's reign contributed significantly to the conditions that resulted in the French Revolution.

Should the writer make this addition here?

- **(A)** Yes, because it provides historical context for the Thorne Miniature Rooms exhibit.
- **(B)** Yes, because it explains why salons are often ornately decorated.
- **(C)** No, because it interrupts the paragraph's description of the miniature salon.
- **(D)** No, because it implies that the interior designer of the salon had political motivations.

Remember, don't look at the Yes/No. Just focus on the "because…" and disprove anything wrong!

Does this added sentence provide some historical context? Sure. Is it historical context for the exhibit? No. It's just some information that happens to be about the same person and diverts into the French Revolution. The entire exhibit is not just this one mini replica. Some of the others are probably not a salon from that time.

Does this added sentence explain why salons are ornately decorated? Nope.

Does it interrupt the description of the salon? Yes.

Does it imply some kind of political motivations? No.

Ask yourself the right questions about each answer choice, and you'll get there.

This exhibit showcases sixty-eight miniature rooms inserted into a wall at eye level. Each furnished room consists of three walls; the fourth wall is a glass pane through which museumgoers observe. The rooms and their furnishings were painstakingly created to scale at 1/12th their actual size, so that one inch in the exhibit correlates with one foot in real life. A couch, for example, is seven inches long, and ⭐ **❼ that is based on a seven-foot-long couch.** ⭐ Each room represents a distinctive style of European, American, or Asian interior design from the thirteenth to twentieth centuries.

❼ Which choice gives a second supporting example that is most similar to the example already in the sentence?

- **(A)** NO CHANGE
- **(B)** a teacup is about a quarter of an inch.
- **(C)** there are even tiny cushions on some.
- **(D)** household items are also on this scale.

This question is asking for a SECOND example. So, ask yourself what the first example was an example of. It was an example of **scale**.

A is just a continuation of the same example, not a new example.

C also mostly just continues the same example.

D is just too vague. It doesn't actually give an **example** of scale.

B is the correct answer.

[1] What was less well-known, until recently at least, was how this relationship among sea otters, sea urchins, and kelp forests might help fight global warming. [2] The amount of carbon dioxide in the atmosphere has increased 40 percent ✶ **26** ✶. [3] A recent study by two professors at the University of California, Santa Cruz, Chris Wilmers and James Estes, **27** suggests, that kelp forests protected by sea otters can absorb as much as twelve times the amount of carbon dioxide from the atmosphere as those where sea urchins are allowed to **28** devour the kelp.

26 At this point, the writer is considering adding the following information.

since the start of the Industrial Revolution, resulting in a rise in global temperatures

Should the writer make this addition here?

(A) Yes, because it establishes the relationship between the level of carbon dioxide in the atmosphere and global warming.
(B) Yes, because it explains the key role sea otters, sea urchins, and kelp forests play in combating global warming.
(C) No, because it contradicts the claim made in the previous paragraph that sea otters help keep kelp forests healthy.
(D) No, because it mentions the Industrial Revolution, blurring the focus of the paragraph.

Does this addition explain anything about sea otters and sea urchins? No.

Does it say anything about sea otters helping to keep kelp forests healthy? No.

Does it mention the Industrial Revolution? Yes. Does that blur the focus of the paragraph? No. This additional bit is giving a time frame and then connecting us to global warming.

A is the answer.

[3] A recent study by two professors at the University of California, Santa Cruz, Chris Wilmers and James Estes, ㉗ **suggests, that** kelp forests protected by sea otters can absorb as much as twelve times the amount of carbon dioxide from the atmosphere as those where sea urchins are allowed to ㉘ devour the kelp.

㉗

    (A) NO CHANGE
    (B) suggests—that
    (C) suggests, "that
    (D) suggests that

Should be simple. Dashes need a pair. Quotes need a pair. And commas don't just go everywhere all willy nilly! I only include this because it's worth repeating yet again!

Answer is D.

[1] What was less well-known, until recently at least, was how this relationship among sea otters, sea urchins, and kelp forests might help fight global warming. [2] The amount of carbon dioxide in the atmosphere has increased 40 percent **26**. [3] A recent study by two professors at the University of California, Santa Cruz, Chris Wilmers and James Estes, **27** suggests, that kelp forests protected by sea otters can absorb as much as twelve times the amount of carbon dioxide from the atmosphere as those where sea urchins are allowed to **28** devour the kelp. [4] Like **29** their terrestrial plant cousins, kelp removes carbon dioxide from the atmosphere, turning it into sugar fuel through photosynthesis, and releases oxygen back into the air. [5] Scientists knew this but did not recognize **30** **how large a role they played** in helping kelp forests to significantly decrease the amount of carbon dioxide in the atmosphere.

30

- **(A)** NO CHANGE
- **(B)** how large a role that it played
- **(C)** how large a role sea otters played
- **(D)** that they played such a large role

This one is a bit of a fun one. The issue is that the "sea otters" haven't been mentioned in forever. So, the word "they" isn't at all clear. Who is "they"? At some point, you have to repeat the name or title of the thing you're discussing, at least every couple of sentences.

So, the answer is C!

[1] What was less well-known, until recently at least, was how this relationship among sea otters, sea urchins, and kelp forests might help fight global warming. [2] The amount of carbon dioxide in the atmosphere has increased 40 percent ㉖. [3] A recent study by two professors at the University of California, Santa Cruz, Chris Wilmers and James Estes, ㉗ suggests, that kelp forests protected by sea otters can absorb as much as twelve times the amount of carbon dioxide from the atmosphere as those where sea urchins are allowed to ㉘ devour the kelp. [4] Like ㉙ their terrestrial plant cousins, kelp removes carbon dioxide from the atmosphere, turning it into sugar fuel through photosynthesis, and releases oxygen back into the air. [5] Scientists knew this but did not recognize ㉚ how large a role they played in helping kelp forests to significantly decrease the amount of carbon dioxide in the atmosphere. ㉛

㉛ Where is the most logical place in this paragraph to add the following sentence?

What Wilmers and Estes discovered in their study, therefore, surprised them.

   (A) After sentence 1
   (B) After sentence 3
   (C) After sentence 4
   (D) After sentence 5

First, we look to see if the paragraph is transitioning FROM one thing TO another thing.

In this case, it isn't. But you should always look for that first, develop that as a habit.

When we see that there is no clear transition in the paragraph, we start to look for key Linking Words. In the added sentence, the word "surprised" at the end tells us that the next sentence should be about…something surprising! The word "therefore" in the middle tells us that this added sentence is an Effect of some Cause that should come just before this sentence.

~So, read through this paragraph again and look for a location that talks about something surprising.

Sentences 5 and 6 are the right stuff. Sentence 5 tells us something that scientists knew, and also something that they "did not recognize". In order to be **surprised**, you must first **not know** the thing. So, when looking for surprise in a passage, you can also look for the some variation of not knowing. That can often be easier to spot.

Then sentence 6 has a bit of a weird construction. It says "far from making no difference to the ecosystem…" and then talks about the huge impact sea otters have. That's telling us that the general knowledge was that sea otters made no difference, but then they discovered that the truth was far away from that. Maybe you didn't pick up on that at first, but think about it. Why mention that is was "far from making no difference"? Why not just say, "Here's the amount of difference sea otters made"?

That added bit serves some purpose. It tells us something NOT true. The only real reason to specifically mention something NOT true is if most people believed that untruth and it needs to be dispelled.

Now, taken together, we have the scientists **not knowing** that sea otters had such a big impact, and then they find out that sea otters have a really big impact. Such a discovery would probably surprise them. (So, the answer is D.)

Lots of students struggle with this question. I think mostly the reason is that this added sentence is unnecessary. Whenever the added sentences are clearly necessary for the logic of the paragraph, you guys do pretty well. But when the added sentence is just something to throw in, your brains read through the paragraph and think, "It doesn't need to go anywhere at all." And that's it. But, in this question, there is no "delete" option. There is no "don't add that sentence" answer choice.

So, recognize that that's something you'll have to combat. Plenty of these added sentences will be totally unnecessary. But, if it must be added, then don't ask yourself where the sentence is needed. Just look for paragraph flow, and then look for Linking Words. Figure out where the sentence **could** make sense.

Planned obsolescence, a practice ㉞ at which products are designed to have a limited period of ㉟ usefulness, has been a cornerstone of manufacturing strategy for the past 80 years. This approach increases sales, but it also stands in ㊱ austere contrast to a time when goods were produced to be durable. Planned obsolescence wastes materials as well as energy in making and shipping new products. It also reinforces the belief that it is easier to replace goods than to mend them, as repair shops are rare and ✶ ㊲ **repair methods are often specialized.** ✶ In 2009, an enterprising movement, the Repair Café, challenged this widely accepted belief.

㊲ Which choice provides information that best supports the claim made by this sentence?

(A) NO CHANGE

(B) obsolete goods can become collectible items.

(C) no one knows whether something will fall into disrepair again.

(D) new designs often have "bugs" that must be worked out.

WHAT IS THE CLAIM?!??

Don't forget to ask yourself that! If you didn't already, go ahead and answer now.

Now, a CLAIM is different from just a simple, ridiculous summary of the paragraph. The paragraph is **about** planned obsolescence. This sentence makes the **claim** that people think it is "easier to replace goods than to mend them". So, we want details explaining how easy it is to replace things or how hard it is to fix them.

There is only one option that talks about that, and that is answer choice A.

I believe you all struggle with this question (and others like it) primarily because you don't actually ask yourselves what the claim is. Which, we have previously discussed, is nonsense! Lol

But, I've also seen, for this question, students who don't realize that you could have EITHER an example talking about how easy it is to replace things OR an example of how hard it is to fix them. Because the sentence talks about the ease of replacing, you only focus on that. You don't see any answer choices about replacing, and then you just wildly pick any answer for either no reason at all, or some nonsense reason that you know is silly.

No judgement. My brain does crazy stuff too. Just be aware of what your brain does in these moments. Explore that line between logic and Mental Gymnastics. Don't make it weird, but don't shut your brain down completely and look rigidly at the words written. You do know how to draw perfectly reasonable, logical conclusions from sentences.

[1] More like a ㊳ fair then an actual café, the first Repair Café took place in Amsterdam, the Netherlands. [2] It was the brainchild of former journalist Martine Postma, ㊴ wanting to take a practical stand in a throwaway culture. [3] Her goals were ㊵ straightforward, however: reduce waste, maintain and perpetuate knowledge and skills, and strengthen community. [4] Participants bring all manner of damaged articles—clothing, appliances, furniture, and more—to be repaired by a staff of volunteer specialists including tailors, electricians, and carpenters. [5] Since the inaugural Repair Café, others have been hosted in theater foyers, community centers, hotels, and auditoriums. [6] While ㊶ they await for service, patrons can enjoy coffee and snacks and mingle with their neighbors in need. ㊷

㊷ To make this paragraph most logical, sentence 5 should be placed

  (A) where it is now.
  (B) before sentence 1.
  (C) after sentence 3.
  (D) after sentence 6.

First, we ask ourselves what the passage is transitioning From and To (ignoring sentence 5, of course).

The paragraph is essentially transitioning from General to Specific, but it's not very clear or very strong. So, we can look for other things to help us out here.

Here's a fun trick: Verb Tense Transition!!

~Find the main verb in each sentence. (Don't include any verbs that are italicized, as those might have been changed in other questions.)

[1] took
[2] was
[3] were
[4] bring
[5] have been
[6] can enjoy...and mingle

~Okay, now write out the tense of each of these verbs.

[1] Past
[2] Past
[3] Past
[4] Present
[5] Past
[6] Present

Pretty cool, right?! Paragraphs will often transition from Past to Present! This isn't as common a transition, but it's worth adding to the memory banks.

From this, we can see that sentence 5 can't go where it is now or after sentence 6. That narrows it down to B or C and B is easily and quickly eliminated due to its total illogic.

Answer is C.

Though only about 3 percent of the Netherlands' municipal waste ends up in landfills, Repair Cafés still raise awareness about what may otherwise be mindless acts of waste by providing a venue for people to share and learn valuable skills that are in danger of being lost.
★ ㊷ ★ It is easy to classify old but fixable items as "junk" in an era that places great emphasis on the next big thing. In helping people consider how the goods they use on a daily basis work and are made, Repair Cafés restore a sense of relationship between human beings and material goods.

㊷ At this point, the writer is considering adding the following sentence.

As the number of corporate and service-based jobs has increased, the need for people who work with their hands has diminished.

Should the writer make this addition here?

    (A) Yes, because it provides an example of specific repair skills being lost.
    (B) Yes, because it elaborates on the statistic about the Netherlands' municipal waste.
    (C) No, because it blurs the paragraph's focus by introducing a topic that is not further explained.
    (D) No, because it contradicts the claims made in the rest of the paragraph.

Disprove; Don't Prove. Focus on the Because...

Does this sentence provide an example of specific repair skills being lost? Nope.

Does this sentence elaborate on the statistic about the Netherlands' municipal waste? No. It's talking about skills now, not waste in landfills.

Does this sentence contradict the claims made in the rest of the paragraph? No. No contradictions of any kind!

So, the answer is C. C is just the generic answer of "No, because it's not a good sentence; it doesn't fit" etc. We're only allowed to pick that kind of answer AFTER we disprove all the others!

If, at this point, you still aren't relying on Disprove; Don't Prove...

I get it. It seems unnecessary. It seems like more work. It seems like actually 3 times more work! Disproving THREE answer choices is more than just proving ONE answer, right? Won't disproving take longer?

Disproving doesn't take much longer, if at all. You have to read all the answer choices anyways. You just go through and make sure that you know why three answer choices are super, duper wrong.

Also, Disproving works…and Proving doesn't. If you bought this book, you probably already tried the "select the correct answer" method…a lot. And, it didn't work for you. I've explained why before. The way you're taught about "proof" for a claim is…wonky at best. And yet, all my students have been **naturally good at disproving**. I work with students all across the country in 5th to 12th grade. Somehow, no matter the age, gender, or geographic location, all my students were naturally good at disproving. (This may have something to do with kids being generally argumentative. Who knows! I certainly was at that age…lol)

So, I get it. You haven't committed yet. When you do, your score will go up. Until you do, you'll still struggle. But, I'll still be here, encouraging you and maybe making fun of you a little and reminding you to Disprove; Don't Prove.

The Rest of the Practice Tests

At this point, you have eight College Board Official practice tests remaining. Tests 1, 3, and 5-10.

If you've already used a lot of those tests and need more, contact me at www.VohraMethod.com/crash-course-resources. I can provide you will a lot more practice tests.

In my Reading Crash Course, I prescribed those remaining tests in a particular order. For Grammar, it doesn't matter what order you complete the tests in. The Grammar section is a lot more straightforward.

Here are the rules for all of the Grammar practice sections you take going forward:

- » You must take them TIMED, obviously. If you're consistently running out of time, you should get in touch with me. That's a whole different issue and needs a targeted approach. It doesn't just "get better" accidentally.

- » You should review the included Grammar Cheat Sheet before taking each practice section. Those are useful reminders for how to annotate productively, what skills to focus on, etc.

- » You must fully, completely review every single wrong question before moving on to the next practice test. You must also review any questions that took you too long, or that you were unsure about.

- » Try not to be too miserable =)

Work hard, and your efforts will pay off!

Appendix A: Your Pre-Test Cheat Sheet

DO NOT look at this during your practice tests. This is a PRE-TEST cheat sheet, not a DURING test cheat sheet, obviously.

Feel free to rip these pages out of this book and carry them with you to your real test!

1. **Look for Clauses.**
   Clauses will inform MOST of your Punctuation questions and many of the Reading Comprehension questions as well.

2. **Disprove; Don't Prove.**
   It's just as important in Grammar as it is in Reading.

3. Keep things simple!

4. DO YOUR VOCAB SYNAPSE!

5. **DO NOT look at the Keep/Discard or the Yes/No.**
   Just look at the "because..."

6. **Use logic!**
   Don't turn your brain off. Remember, the Grammar section is very much about Reading.

7. **Transition Words**
   Cause and Effect
   More information
   Compare/Contrast
   Example

8. Focus on the Verb in every sentence.

9. **Ask yourself questions!**
   What details should this contain?
   What is this transitioning from and to?
   What should this information be adding?
   Things like that. Talk to yourself, a lot!

10. **What is the paragraph transitioning FROM and TO? What is the sentence transitioning FROM and TO?**

    Cause to Effect
    Problem to Solution
    General to Specific
    Linear Progression of Events

    Then, decide if each sentence is part of the From or part of the To.

11. **For Subject-Verb Agreement**, look for Subjects and Verbs that are far from each other.

12. **For Dangling Modifiers**, make sure the leading modifier is touching the word that it modi-fies.

13. **For Pronoun-Antecedent Agreement**, look for Pronouns and Antecedents that are far from each other.

14. **Redundancy and Brevity** are pretty common. Look for those on the regular!

15. In general, with **commas** surrounding some extra information, you only use commas if the in-formation is unnecessary for the sentence to make sense. Try taking out the commas and see if the sentence still makes sense or if the person described becomes too vague.

16. **For Comma Such As**, see if the sentence would make sense without the "such as…" addi-tion. If so, you use commas (because the info is unnecessary). If not, then no commas.

17. **For Semicolons**, you need to focus solely on Clauses!

18. **Colons** introduce things, but they are sometimes used weirdly on the SAT. So, focus on dis-proving if it looks weird.

19. **Parentheses and Dashes** ALWAYS come in pairs, but sometimes the pair is far apart.

20. **Charts** will usually disprove three of the four answer choices. Just read the charts and focus on disproving!

21. **For vocab questions,** you can ask yourself what context you'd see a particular word in.

22. Make flashcards for all words you don't know as you're going through these practice tests.

23. On the test, **if you don't know a word, just skip it and hope that's not it.**

    Focus on disproving the other answer choices. If you like one of the other three choices, pick that one. DO NOT just pick the one you don't know because you think the answer is always something you don't know. There's no reason to do that. Just use your skills of disproving, and you'll be fine.

    IF you disprove all the other three, then pick the one word you don't know. But ONLY then!

The best way to get better at Reading and Grammar is to read good books.

So, read lots of good books.

Now, I don't mean books that **other people** say are good. Other people are often wrong and always different from you. They aren't you. You're you. You get to say what books are good **to you**.

So, find books that you like. Read a chapter, and then throw the book out if you don't like it. Read half a chapter; I don't care. Read something and keep trying to find a book that you like. Then, find a genre that you like, an author you like. Grow, in yourself, a love of reading, because people who are great are always readers.

Reading matters in every field and for everyone. And yes, I know I'm standing on a soap box. This is my soap box. I want you to be a reader because it will change your life for the better; there's no doubt in my mind.

I hope you make the time to find books you love. And if you don't, I'll still be here with all the love in the world, reminding you that you should.

Appendix B: Advice

In this section, I'll address some of the most common questions my students ask about studying for the SAT and performing well on test day.

Resting the Brain & "Accurate" Preparation

A lot of students come to me with questions like this:

- » Should I intentionally **not** do any studying the day before the test?
- » Should I do some practice tests early in the morning on a Saturday (around the same time as the real test)?
- » Do I have to take full 4-hour practice tests all at once?
- » Should I change my sleep schedule so I can get used to waking up early in the morning?
- » What do I do if I'm tired on the day of the test?

To all questions of this type, I have one clear response: **You never forget English**.

If I woke you up in the middle of the night and asked you to read a book aloud, you could do it. You might be groggy for the first few minutes, but you wouldn't suddenly forget all the words.

If you stayed up all night long with no sleep, and I handed you a test on basic addition in the morning, you could do it. You would almost certainly be tired, but you wouldn't forget that 2+2=4.

That's what real knowledge is. When you KNOW something, you know it. You know your mom's name. You know how old you are. You know that that thing with four legs and a floofy tail that's bounding at you with love is called a "dog". You don't really forget things that you KNOW.

Student: But Chelsey, I don't KNOW advanced Calculus.

Me: Good point, dear student. If you don't know something so well that you could do it when groggy or really hungry or cold or whatever...then you don't KNOW that thing. For the SAT, you need to KNOW your grammar, KNOW your reading, and KNOW your algebra.

If you KNOW those things, you'll be fine. If you don't KNOW those things, then no amount of extra sleep is going to help you. No altered sleep schedule, no amount of mental rest will make the difference.

That said, **here are a few things I do recommend**:

» When taking practice tests, **do whatever practice you can in the time that you have.** If you have time for just one section of math, do that. If you have time for the full Verbal section (reading & grammar), then do that. If you can make the time for a full test, do that. Just practice. Don't not practice. And definitely don't hold out until you can get that "perfect" study session into your busy schedule. Life isn't about perfect. Life is about showing up.

» **Obviously, get good sleep the night before!** You should get good sleep as many nights of your life as you possibly can. Good sleep is just so obviously necessary for brain development, healing, memory storage, bodily health, emotional health, and a billion other aspects of your life. So yes, get good sleep the night before and all other nights forever.

» If you're worried about waking up, **plan a quick workout.** Just some push ups, jumping jacks, bodyweight squats, whatever. You don't have to go crazy here. But, working out and getting your blood flowing is, in my experience, the best way to wake up your brain and clear the fog.

- **Don't start experimenting with coffee and energy drinks, and don't create brand new life schedules right now.** Now is not the time to introduce new variables into your routine. Just stick with what you know.

- **Keep doing your Vocab Synapse.** Remember, on test day, you cannot "logic" your way through a word you simply don't know. One day of Vocab Synapse training could be the difference between a 1490 and a 1500, or a 1530 and a 1550. At worst, you learned a few more words. At best, you bought yourself 10 to 20+ extra points on the SAT. It's a no-brainer.

- **On the day before your test, keep studying…or don't.** If you've gotten through a lot of the suggested material in this book, then take a day off. If you haven't, then maybe keep studying. But, tou don't need a million tools; you just need to use the few tools you have, and know the few punctuation and selected skills rules you've learned in this book. Once you have those tools and you're automatically relying on them in practice tests, you're good.

Test Day

The questions here are usually something like this:

- » What do I do if I don't know something on the actual test?
- » What do I do if I get really anxious and doubt myself on test day?
- » What do I do if I don't know a word on the actual test?

The general answer is this: **On test day, you know what you know.** There is absolutely nothing you can do to magically know more than you know while you are taking a closed-book, monitored exam. So, your job is to learn as much as you possibly can before that day. Plain and simple.

One extra note:

If you don't understand a particular part of a grammar passage, or a particular vocab word, just ignore it and hope really hard that it's not important for any of the questions.

That might sound like weird advice, but what else can you do? You can't make yourself magically know it simply by stressing out enough... So, ignore it. Or, pick out any of the words in the sentence or paragraph that you DO understand and use those.

Remember your rules. Remember your tactics. Remember to ask yourself questions and engage with what you do know in the passage.

If you don't know ONE thing, all is not lost! Just keep going. If you get that one question wrong, fine. You can get all the other ones right, IF you don't work yourself up into a panic.

Just commit to what you've learned in this book and think it out.

Getting a High Enough Score

So many students ask me some variation of the question, "What do I do if I don't get a high enough score?"

I'll be honest, this question does confuse me a little. Personally, I'm a very stubborn individual. If I don't get what I want, I'm going to keep trying to get it...until I get it. If I want a perfect score, I'll take the test as many times as it takes to get that perfect score. (And no, colleges won't judge you poorly if you took the test several times and continued to **improve** your score. That just shows hard work, diligence, personal desire to improve and grow, etc.)

So, that's what I would do. That's also what I'll tell you to do.

Yes, I know, you don't WANT to take it more than once. You don't want to take it at all, probably. But you probably do want to get into some particular college that has some particular SAT score minimum or average or whatever. So, keep working until you get the score you need. It's that simple.

There is no magic here. It's just hard work, real learning, and very empowering success.

CPSIA information can be obtained
at www.ICGtesting.com
Printed in the USA
BVHW061323030621
608739BV00001B/93